for 1000+ tutorials ... use our
free site .... drawinghowtodraw.com

BY RACHEL GOLDSTEIN

HOW TO DRAW KAWAII CUTE ANIMALS + CHARACTERS

Collection Books 1-3: Easy to Draw Anime and Manga Drawing for Kids

CARTOONING FOR KIDS + LEARNING HOW TO DRAW SUPER CUTE KAWAII ANIMALS CHARACTERS DOODLES & THINGS

LETTER V ICE CREAM

1.

2. #8 Shape

3. Letter E Shapes

4. Letter Y Shape

Letter j Shapes

Letter C Shape

5. Letter U Ears

#3 Shapes

6. Letter V Tail + Letter U Arms

NOW YOU TRY

LETTER U UNICORN

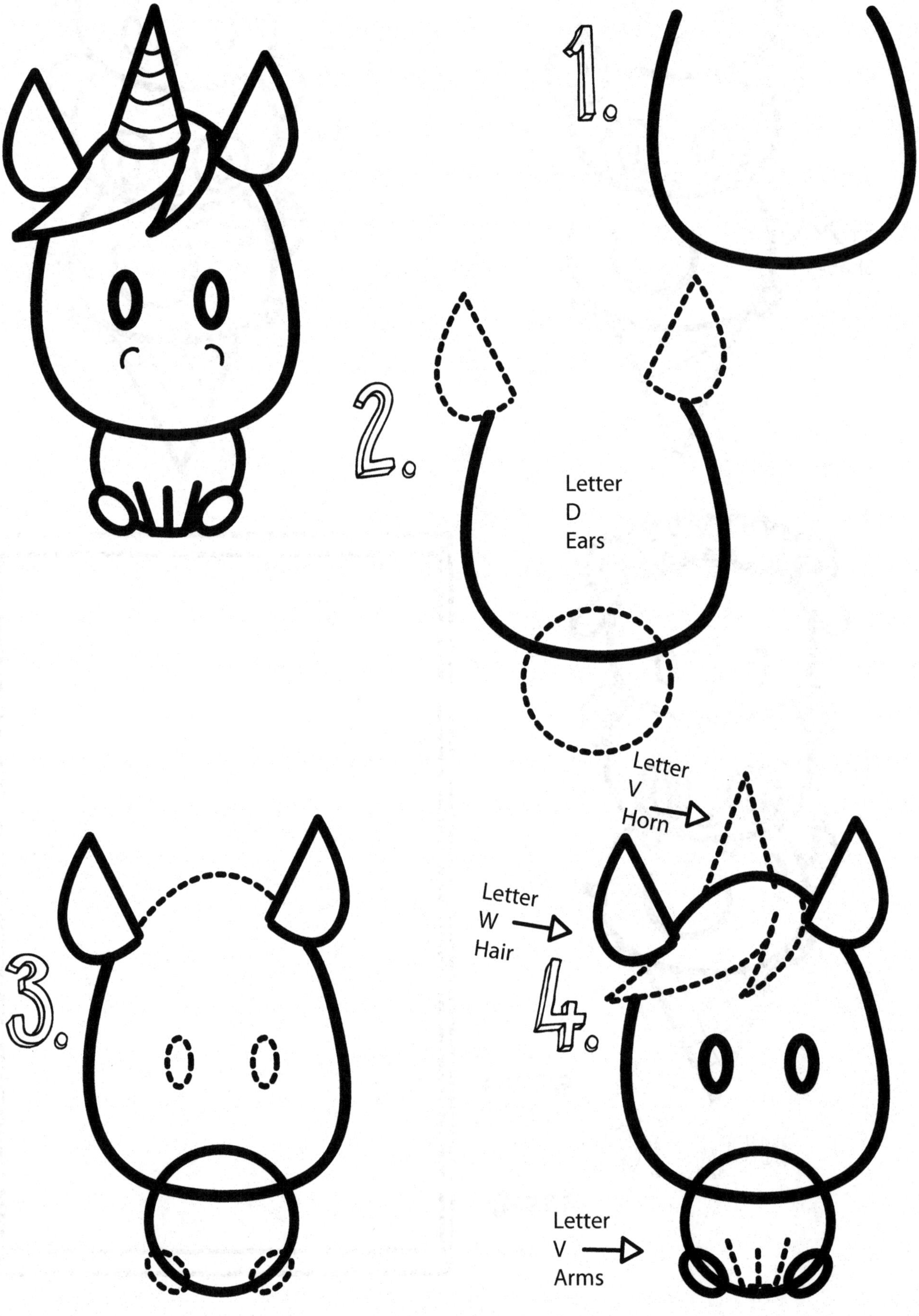

1.

2.

Letter
D
Ears

Letter
V
Horn

3.

Letter
W
Hair

4.

Letter
V
Arms

5.

NOW YOU TRY

LETTER @ HAMSTER

1.

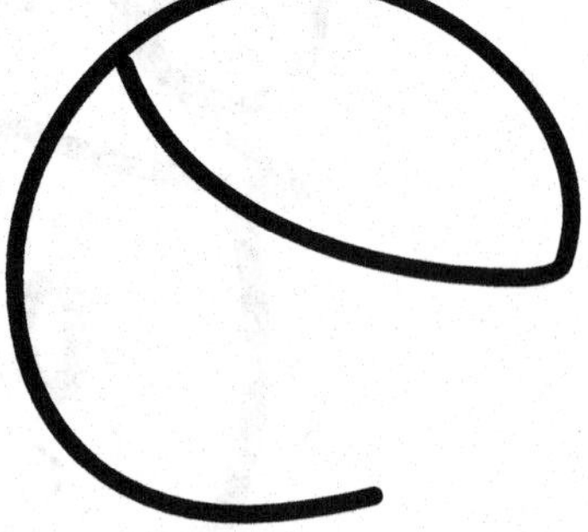

2.

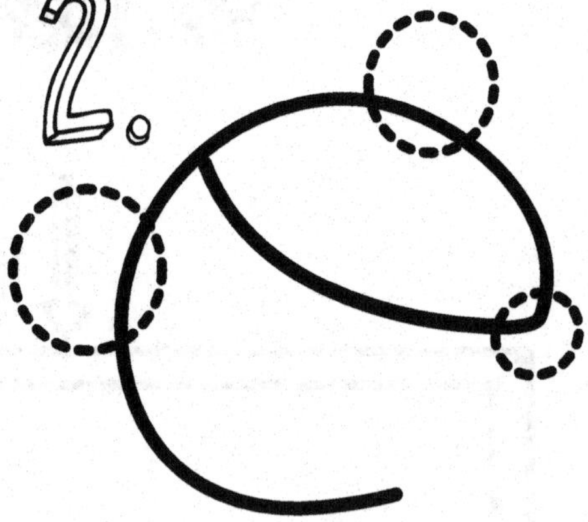

Letter
Y
Shapes

3.

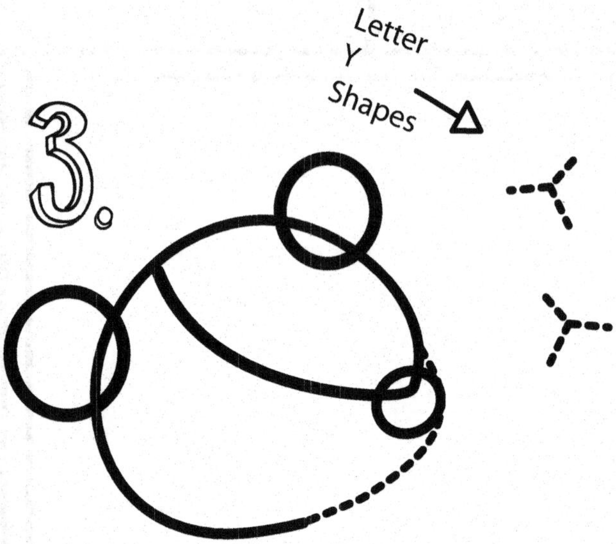

4.

Question
Mark
Shape

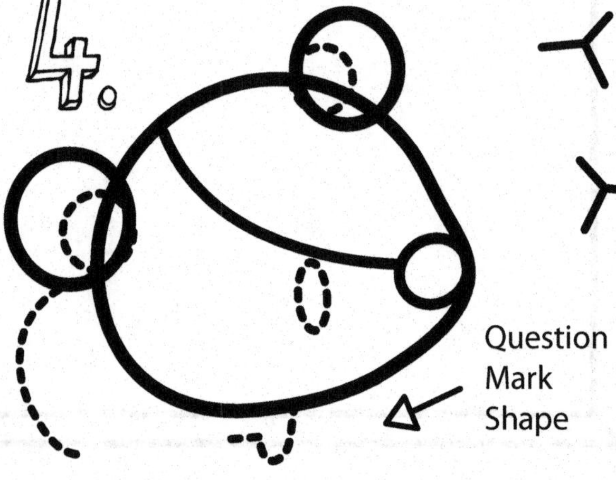

5.

6.

#3 Shapes

Question
Mark
Shape

NOW YOU TRY

NUMBER 3 RACCOON

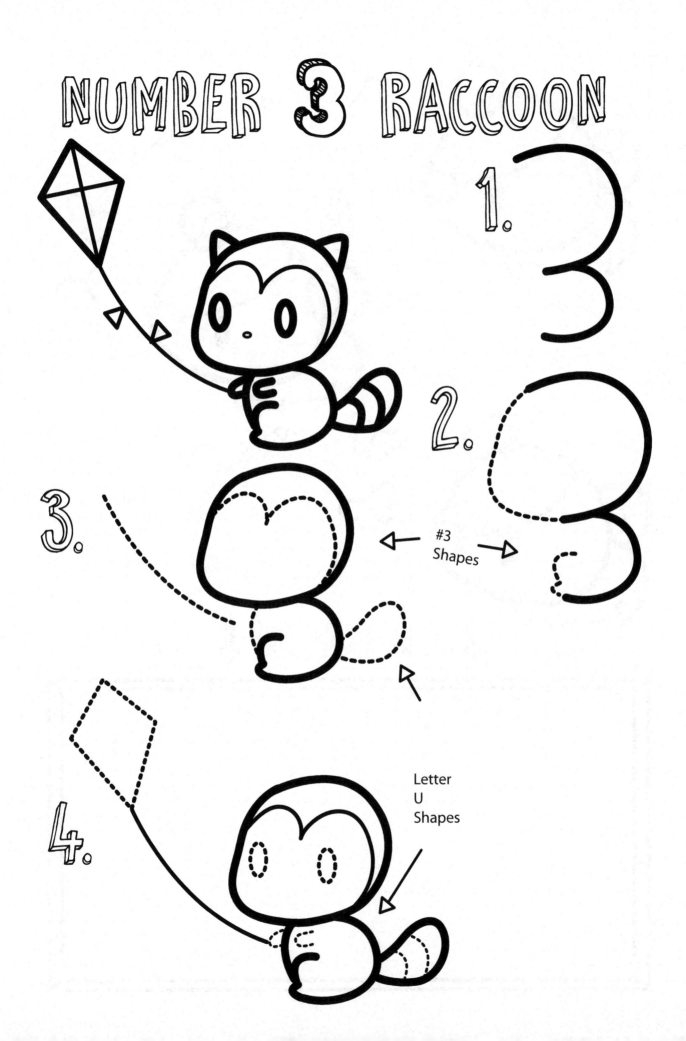

1.

2.

#3 Shapes

3.

4.

Letter U Shapes

5.

Letter V Ears

LETTER F ELEPHANT

1.

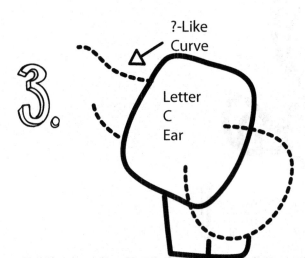

2.

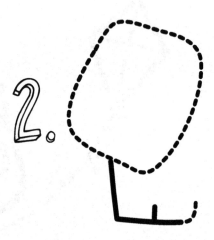

3.

?-Like
Curve

Letter
C
Ear

4.

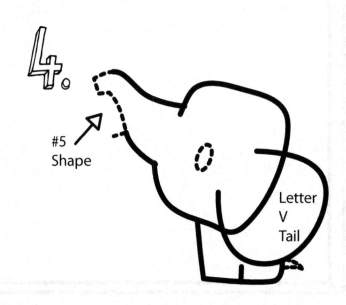

#5
Shape

Letter
V
Tail

NOW YOU TRY

LETTER H MILK CARTON

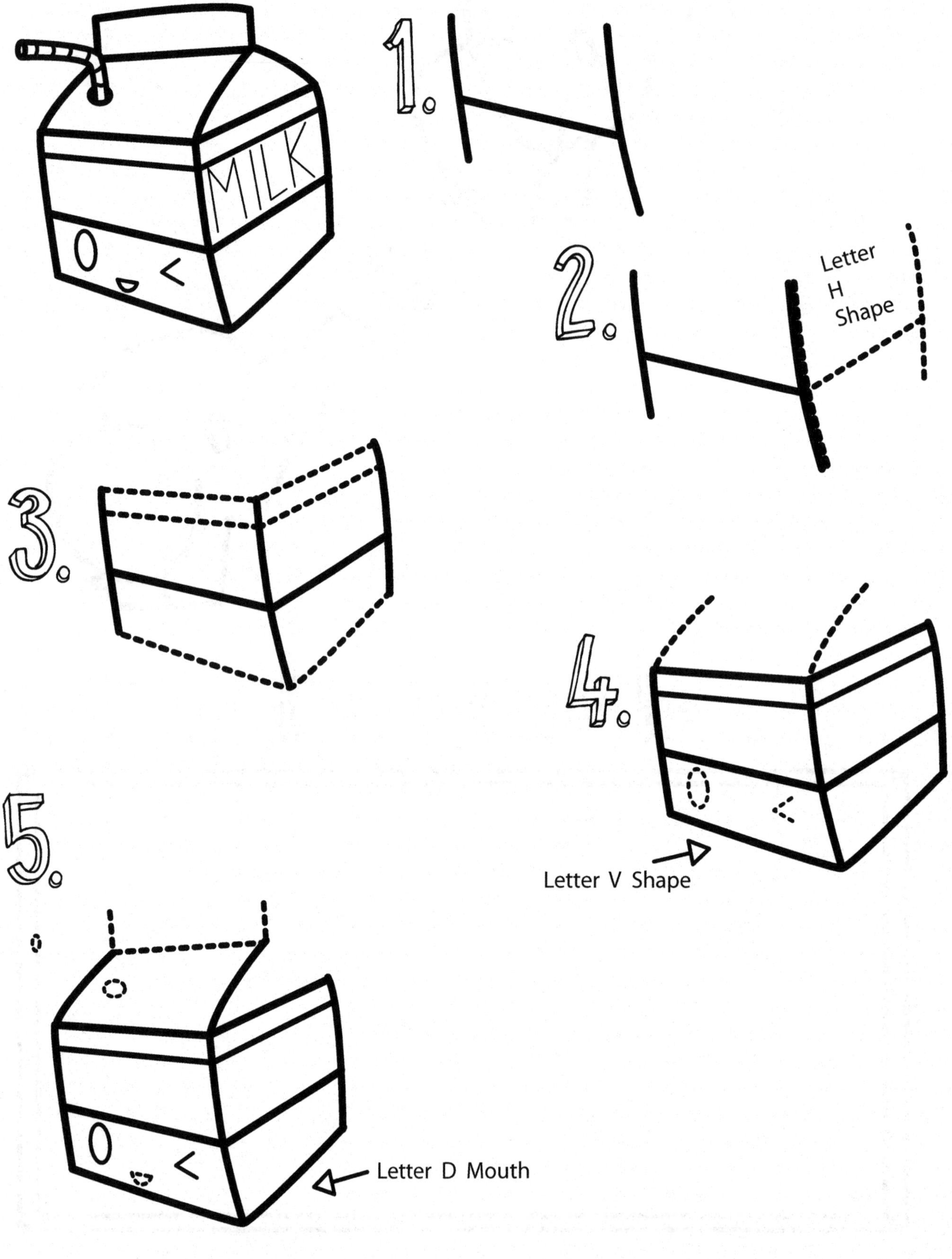

1.

2. Letter H Shape

3.

4. Letter V Shape

5. Letter D Mouth

MILK

6.

7.

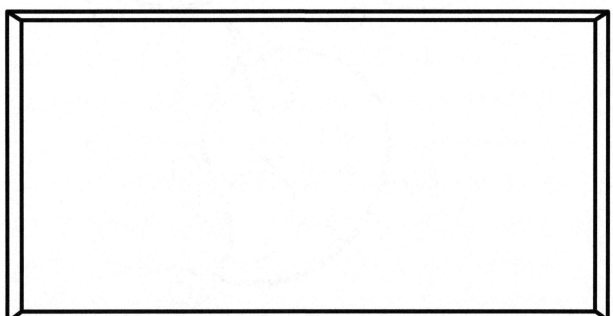

↓ NOW YOU TRY ↓

? SYMBOL NARWHAL

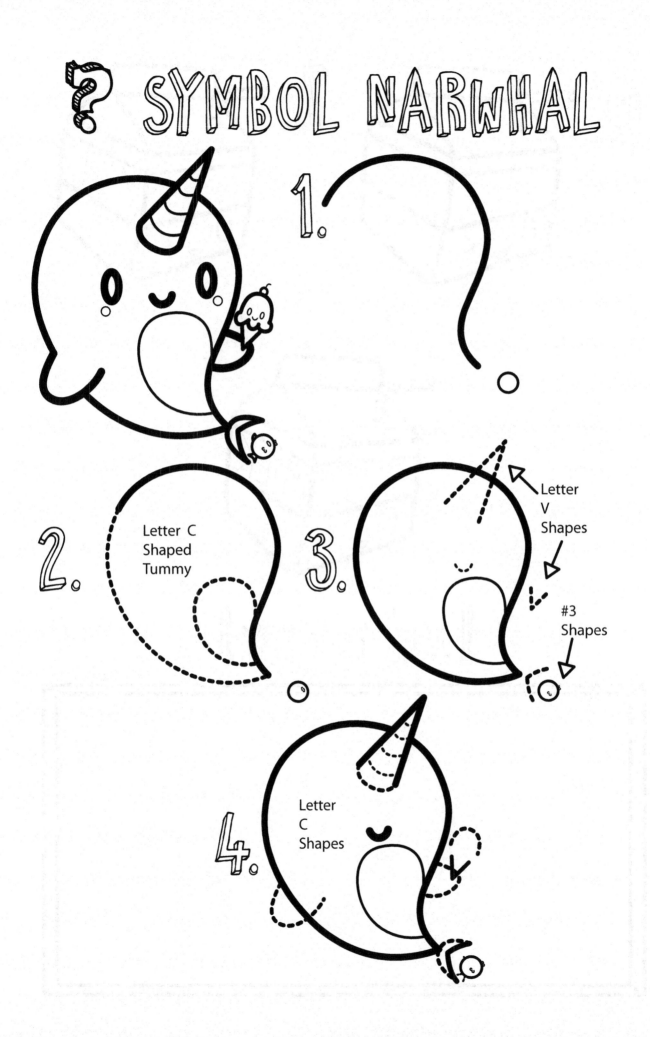

1.

2. Letter C Shaped Tummy

3. Letter V Shapes

#3 Shapes

4. Letter C Shapes

5.

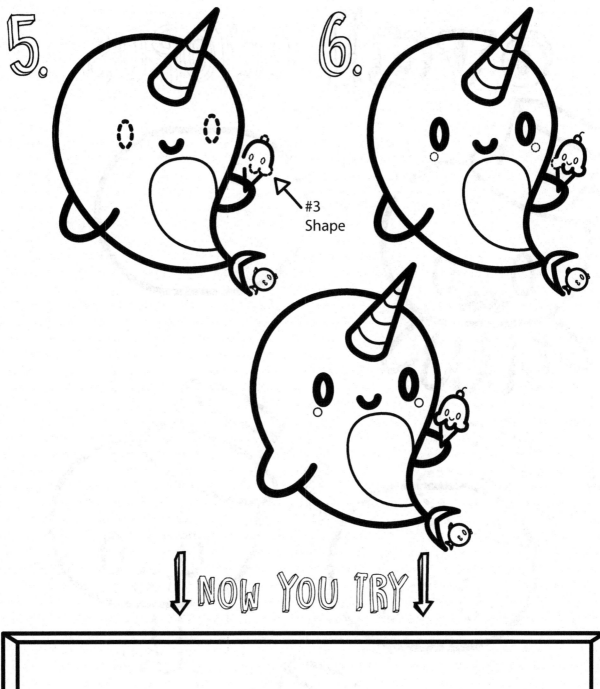

#3
Shape

6.

↓ NOW YOU TRY ↓

oval OCTOPUS

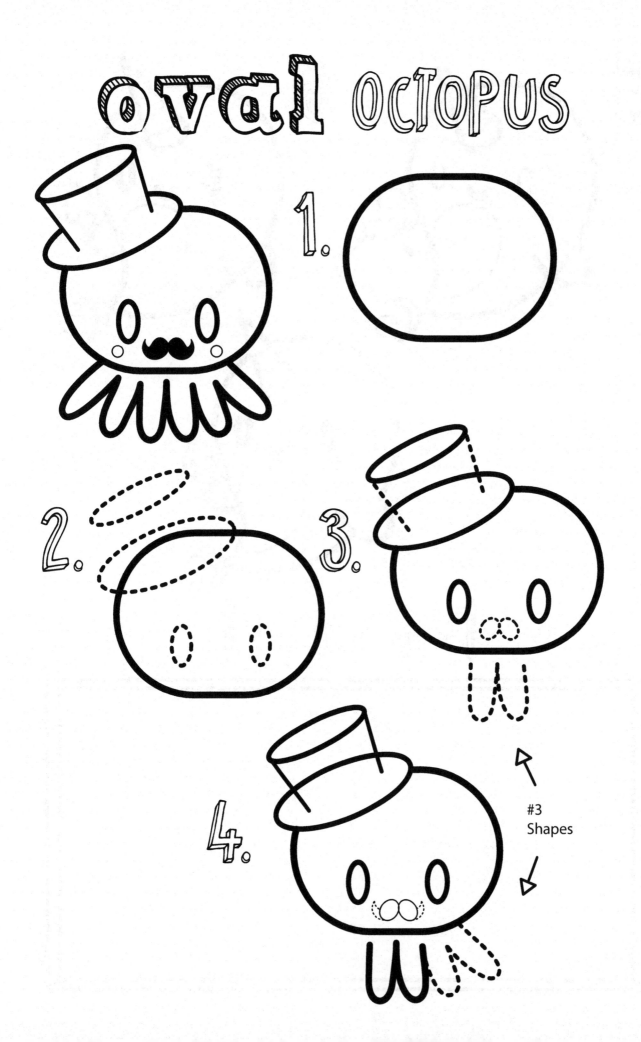

1.

2.

3.

4.

#3 Shapes

5.

#3
Shape

NOW YOU TRY

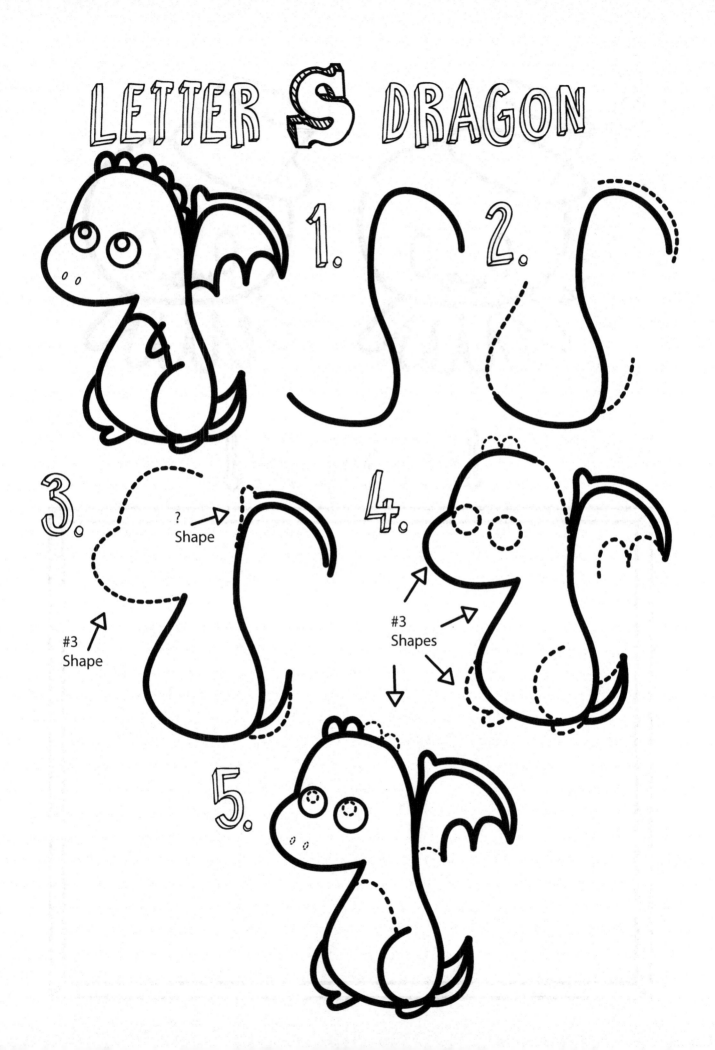

LETTER S DRAGON

1.

2.

3.

? Shape

#3 Shape

4.

#3 Shapes

5.

6.

#3
Shape

Letter
U
Arm

NOW YOU TRY

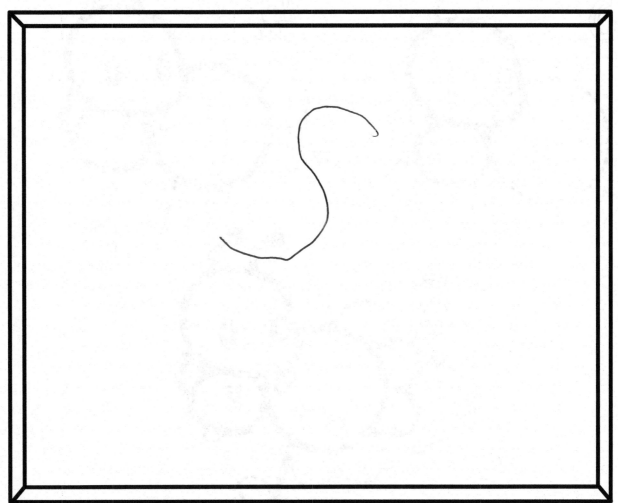

NUMBER 3 BEE

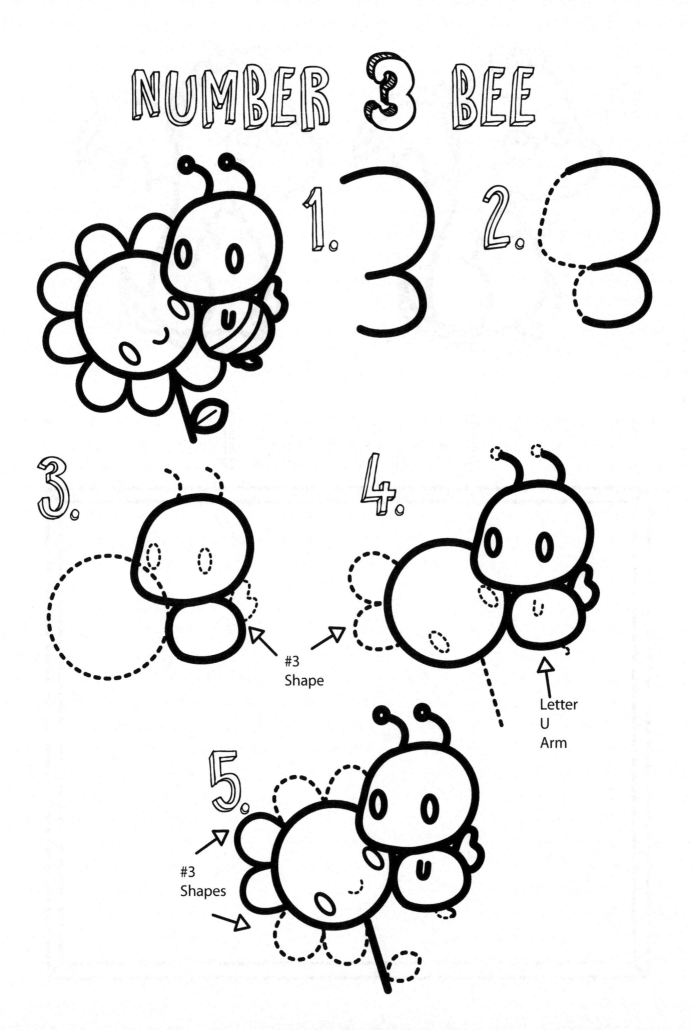

1.

2.

3.

#3
Shape

4.

Letter
U
Arm

5.

#3
Shapes

6.

⇓ NOW YOU TRY ⇓

NUMBER 8 TURTLE

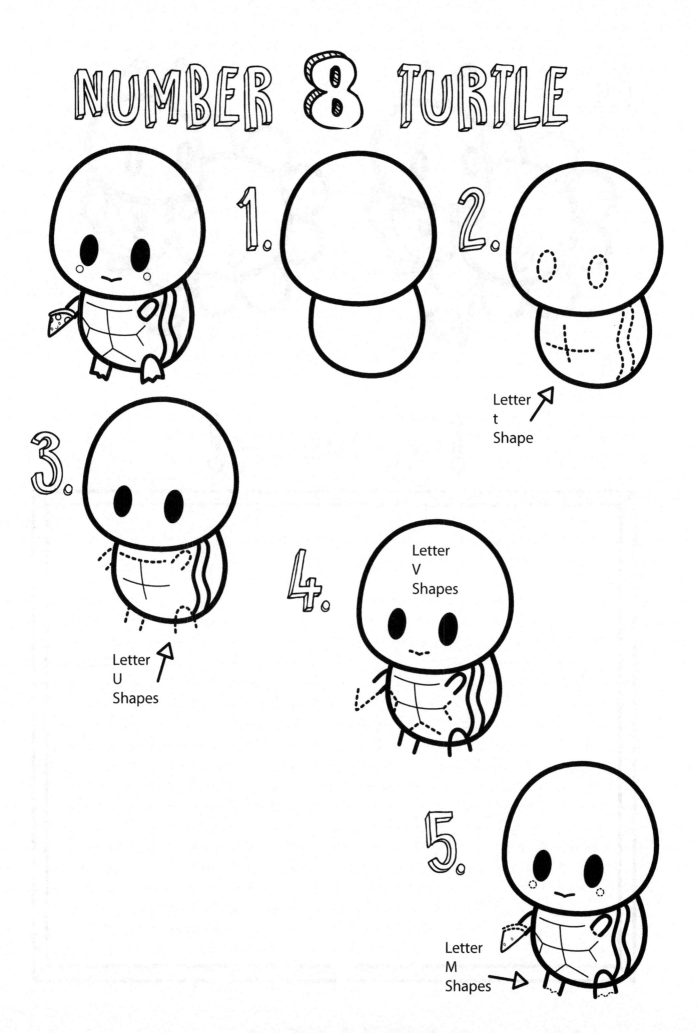

1.

2.

Letter
t
Shape

3.

Letter
U
Shapes

4.

Letter
V
Shapes

5.

Letter
M
Shapes

6.

↓ NOW YOU TRY ↓

NUMBER 6 HAPPY CAT

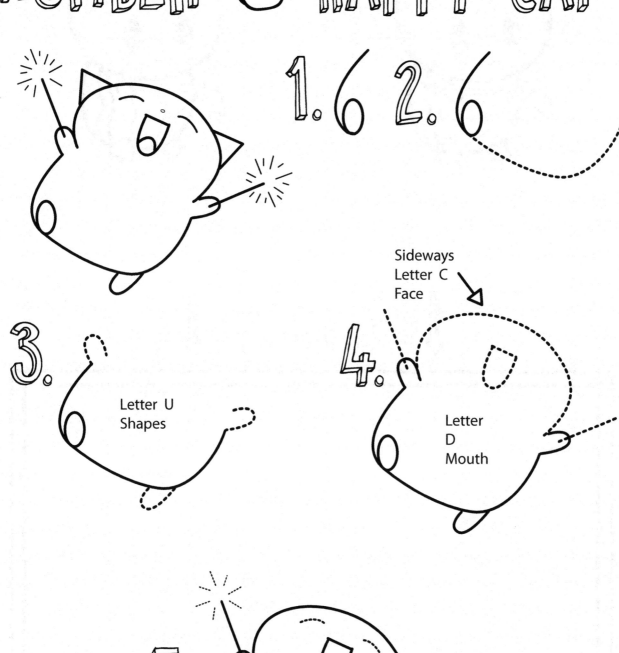

1.6 2.6

Sideways
Letter C
Face

3.

Letter U
Shapes

4.

Letter
D
Mouth

5.

6.

Letter
V
Ears

NOW YOU TRY

oval LIZARD

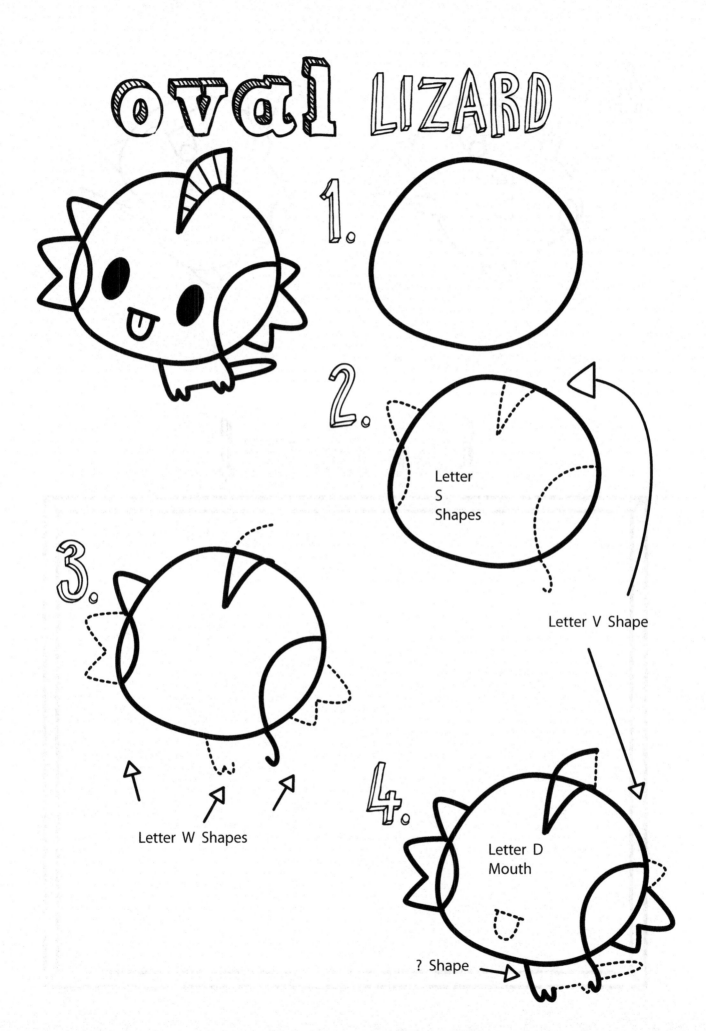

1.

2.
Letter
S
Shapes

Letter V Shape

3.
Letter W Shapes

4.
Letter D
Mouth

? Shape

5.

NOW YOU TRY

NUMBER 8 PENGUINS

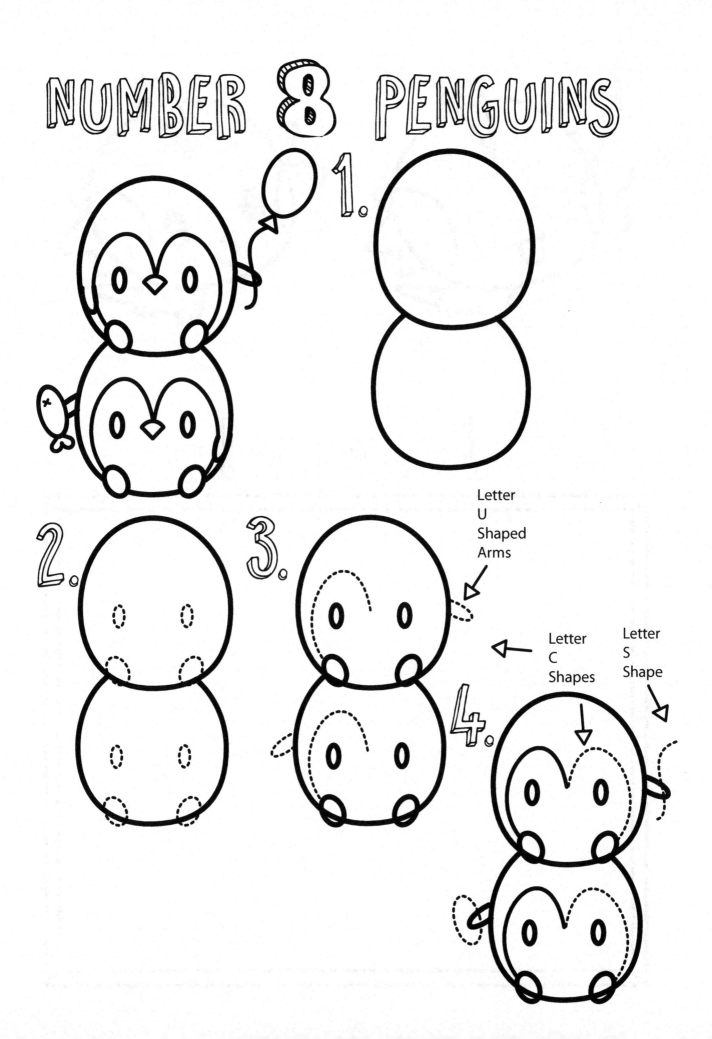

1.

2.

3.

Letter
U
Shaped
Arms

Letter
C
Shapes

Letter
S
Shape

4.

5.

Letter
V
Beaks

#3
Shape

6.

Letter
x
Fish
Eye

↓ NOW YOU TRY ↓

LETTER E HERO

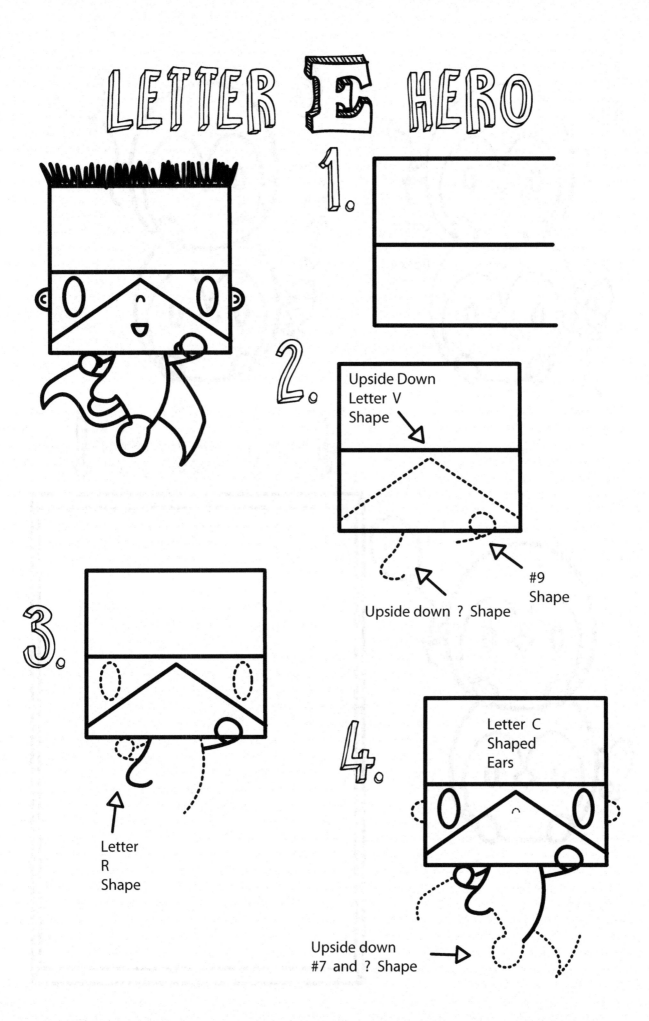

1.

2. Upside Down Letter V Shape

Upside down ? Shape

#9 Shape

3. Letter R Shape

4. Letter C Shaped Ears

Upside down #7 and ? Shape

5.

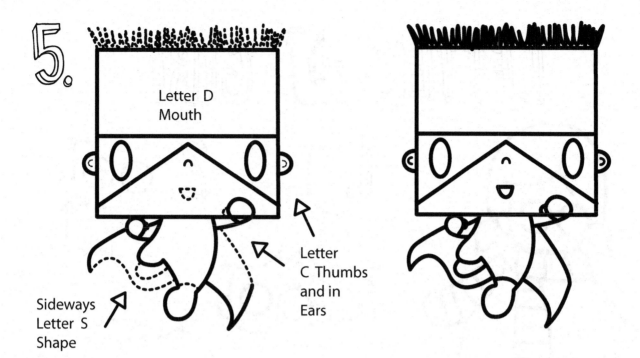

Letter D
Mouth

Sideways
Letter S
Shape

Letter
C Thumbs
and in
Ears

⬇ NOW YOU TRY ⬇

LETTER J GIRL

1. J

2. Letter C Ears

3. Letter T Shape
Letter U Pony tails

4. Letter U Head
Letter V on Pony Tails
Sideways Letter A

5. #3 Shape

6. ! Shape

7.

#2
Shape

8.

#3 Shape

NOW YOU TRY

LETTER U POPSICLE

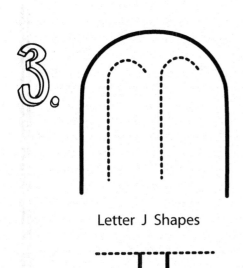

1. U

2.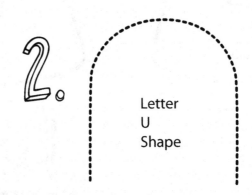
Letter
U
Shape

U

3. Letter J Shapes

4.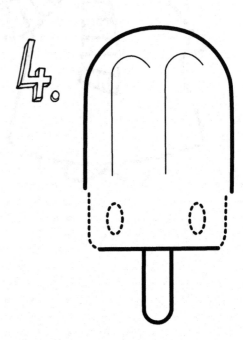

5.

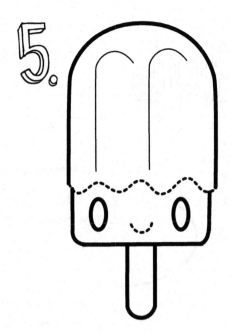

↓ NOW YOU TRY ↓

LETTER C HUG

1.

2. Letter C and M Shapes

3. Letter N Shape

4. #5 Shape   ? Shape

5. #2 Shapes

6. Letter S Shapes in Ears   ? Shape

7. Letter L Shape

8.

9.

NOW YOU TRY

LETTER B COLD BIRDS

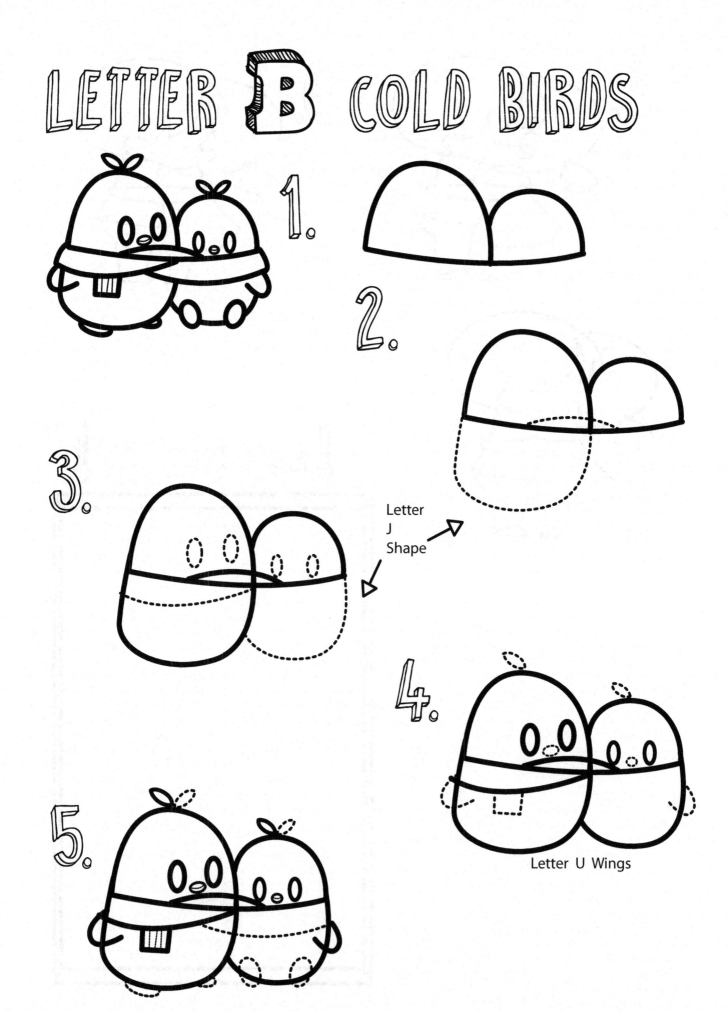

1.

2.

3.

Letter
J
Shape

4.

Letter U Wings

5.

6.

NOW YOU TRY

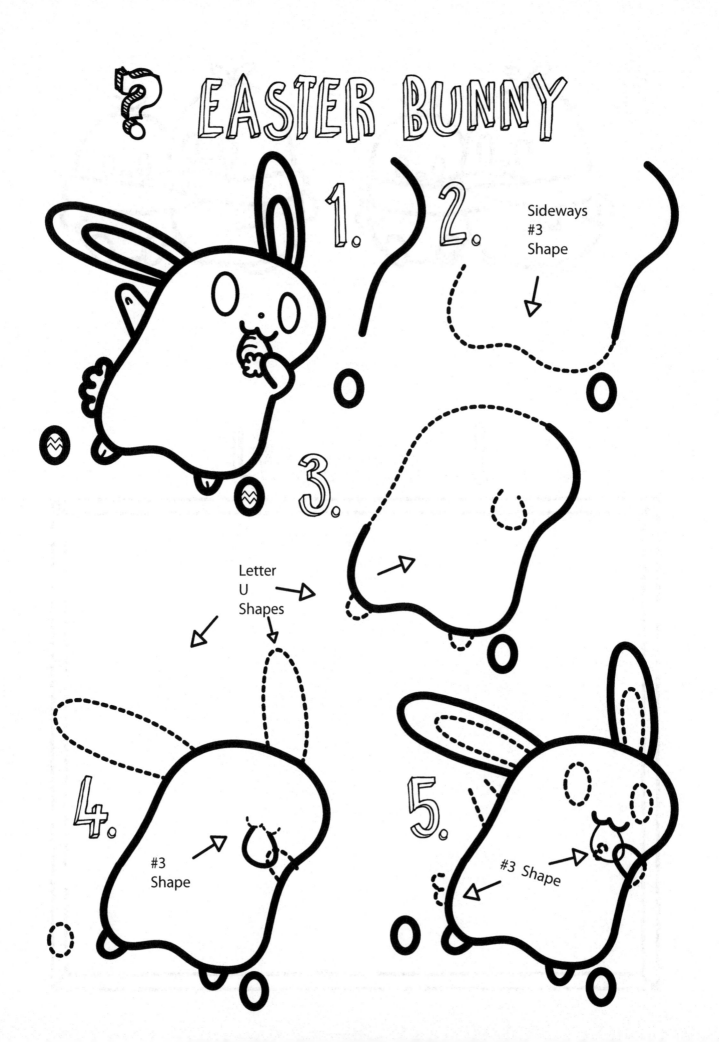

6.

#3 Shape

7.

#3 Shape

Letter M Shapes

NOW YOU TRY

NUMBER PIGGIES

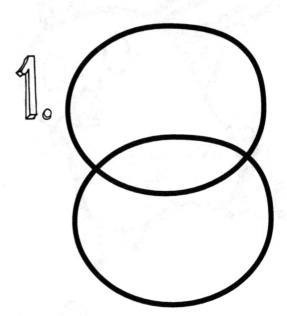

1.

2.

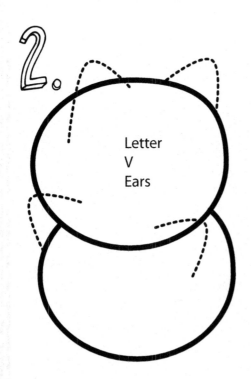

Letter
V
Ears

3.

Cursive
Lowercase
Letter
e
Shapes
for
Tails

4.

5.

↓ NOW YOU TRY ↓

LETTER M KITTIES

1.

2.

3. Letter V Ears

4. Letter V Whiskers

#9 Spiral Shape

5. #3 Mouths

6.

Letter C and Question Mark Shaped Legs

↓ NOW YOU TRY ↓

NUMBER BEAR

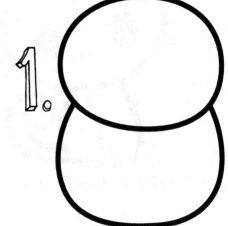

1.

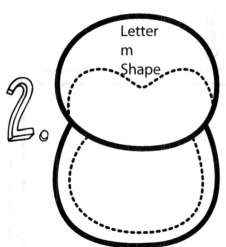

2.

Letter m Shape

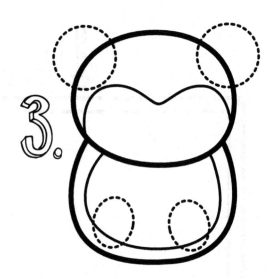

3.

4.

5.

#3 Mouth

Letter U Shaped Arms and Nails

↓ NOW YOU TRY ↓

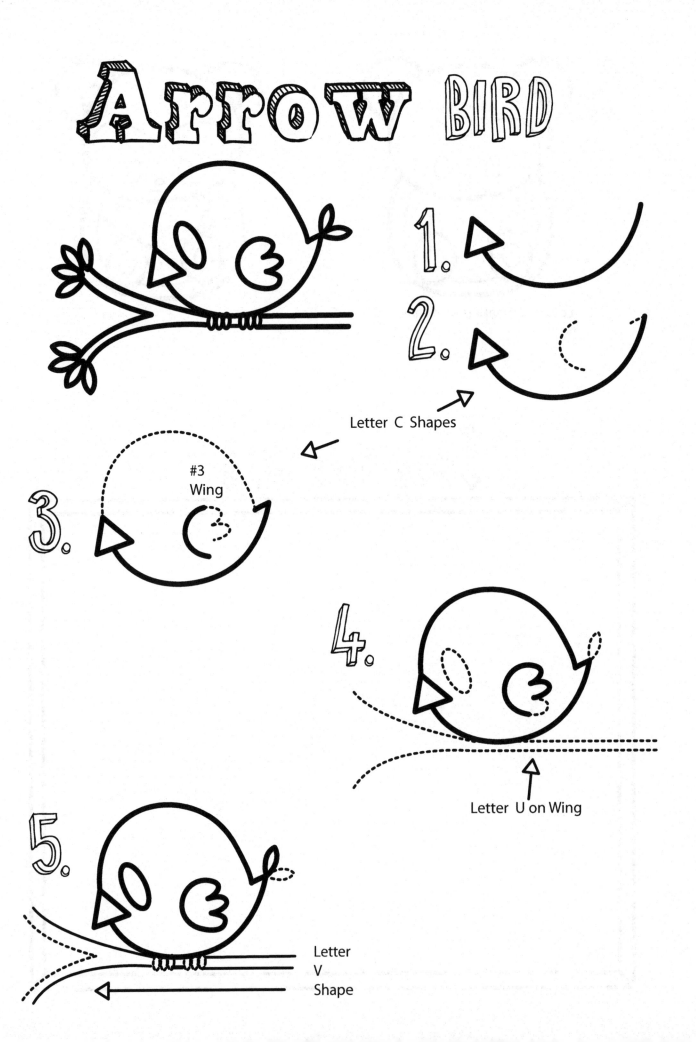

Arrow BIRD

1.

2.

Letter C Shapes

3.

#3
Wing

4.

Letter U on Wing

5.

Letter
V
Shape

6.

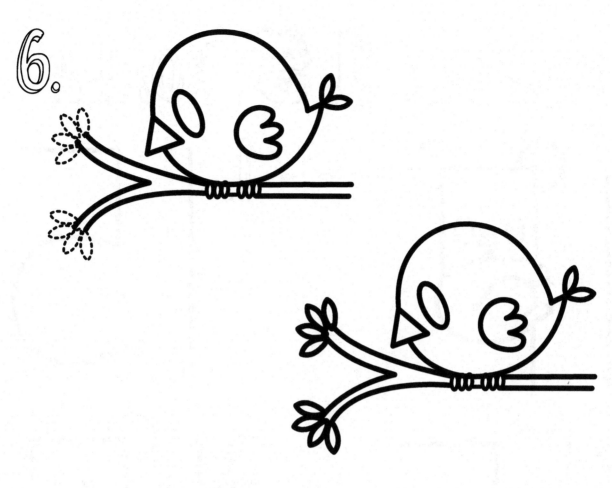

↓ NOW YOU TRY ↓

NUMBER 15 KOALA

1.

2.

3.

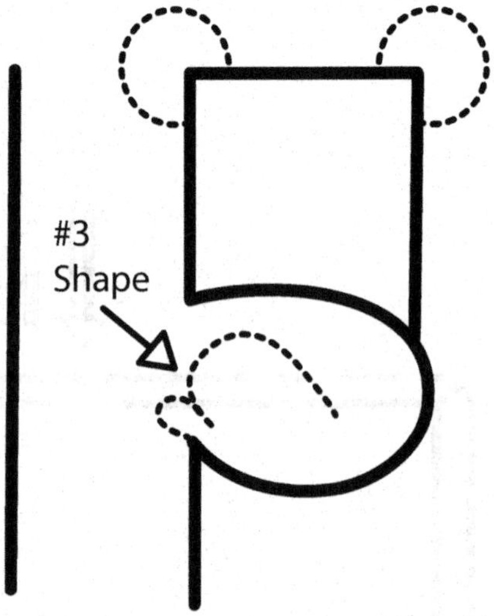

#3
Shape

4.

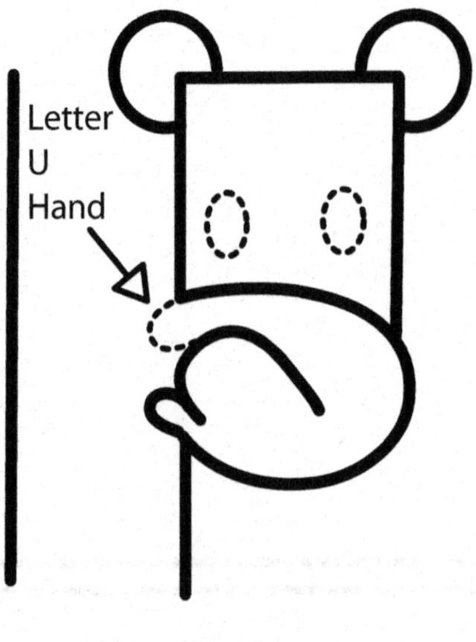

Letter
U
Hand

5.

Letter
V
Nails

NOW YOU TRY

NUMBER 12 PENGUIN

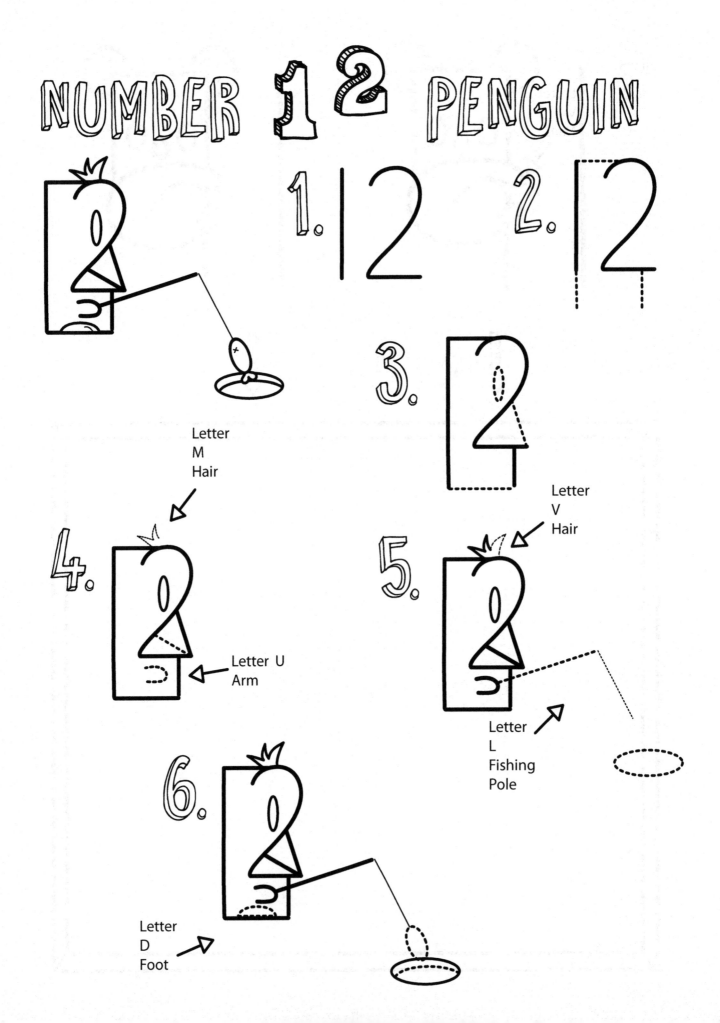

1.

2.

3.

Letter
M
Hair

Letter
V
Hair

4.

Letter U
Arm

5.

Letter
L
Fishing
Pole

6.

Letter
D
Foot

7.

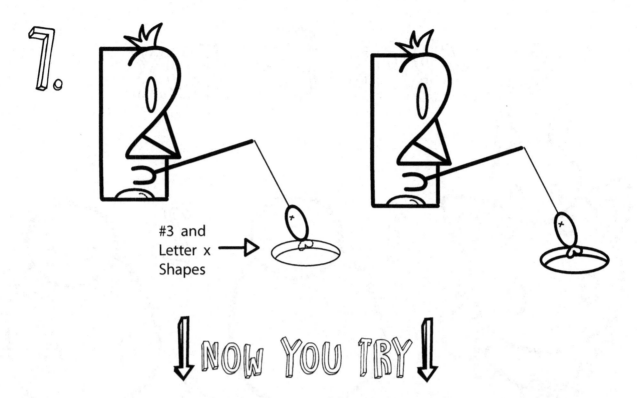

#3 and Letter x Shapes →

↓ NOW YOU TRY ↓

NUMBER 8 FOX

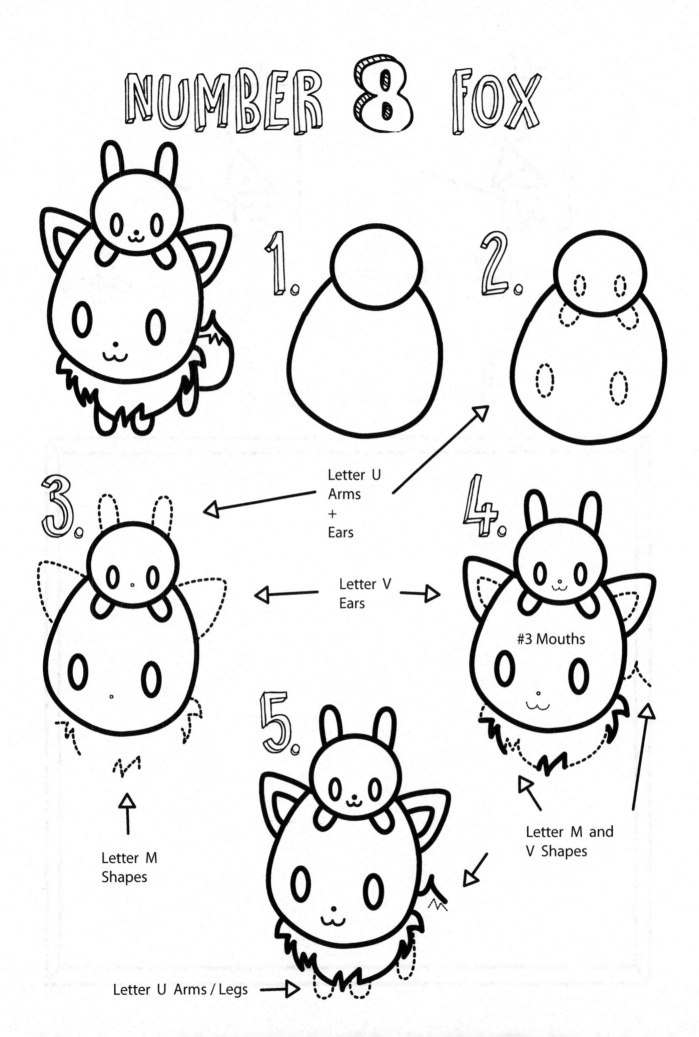

1.

2.

Letter U
Arms
+
Ears

3.

Letter V
Ears

4.

#3 Mouths

5.

Letter M
Shapes

Letter M and
V Shapes

Letter U Arms / Legs

6.

NOW YOU TRY

KISSING KITTIES

1.

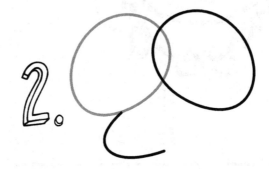

2.

Letter "V" ears

Erase on dotted line

3.

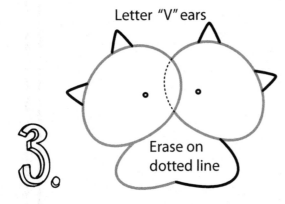

Don't draw the dotted line

4.

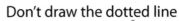

"?" shaped tails

Letter "V" shape

5.

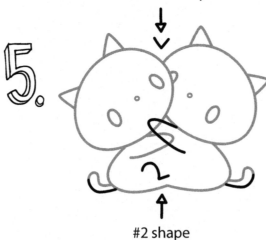

#2 shape

6.

#3 shapes

Backwards #2 shape

Erase
on
dotted
lines

7.

NOW YOU TRY

LLAMA UNICORN

1. Draw cloud shapes. Don't draw the dotted lines.

2.

3.

Draw letter "U" shapes

Draw letter "m" and "v" shapes →

4.

5.

Draw letter "Y" shape

6.

Erase on dotted lines

NOW YOU TRY

SPUNKY CACTUS

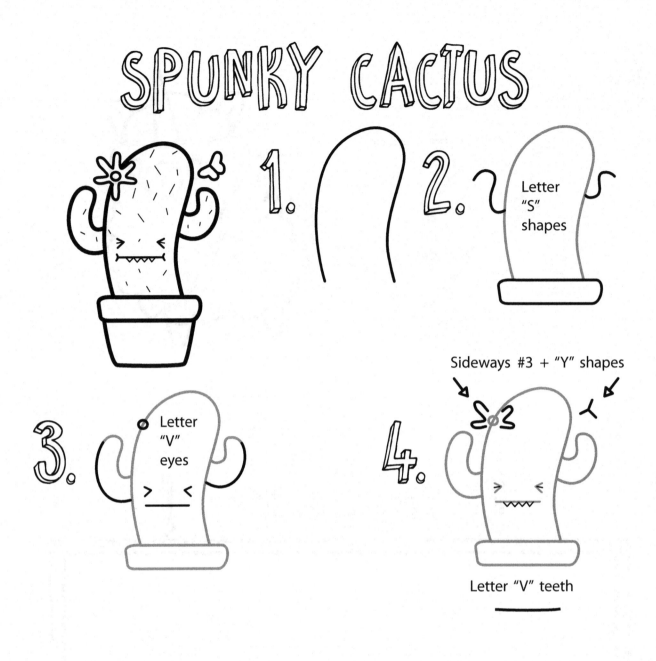

1.

2. Letter "S" shapes

3. Letter "V" eyes

4. Sideways #3 + "Y" shapes

Letter "V" teeth

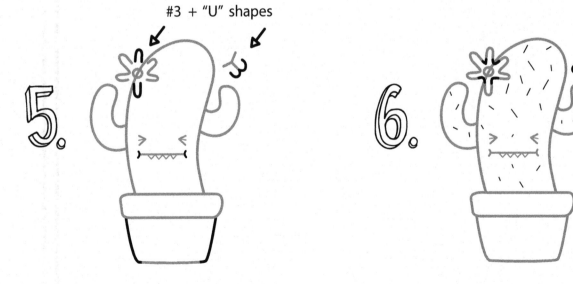

5. #3 + "U" shapes

6.

7.

Erase on dotted line

NOW YOU TRY

GIDDY CHIPMUNK

 1.

Draw a backwards "?" shape

 2.

3.

Don't draw the dotted lines

4.

Draw letter "U" arms

5.

Letter
"W"
shape

NOW YOU TRY

KID IN DRAGON COSTUME

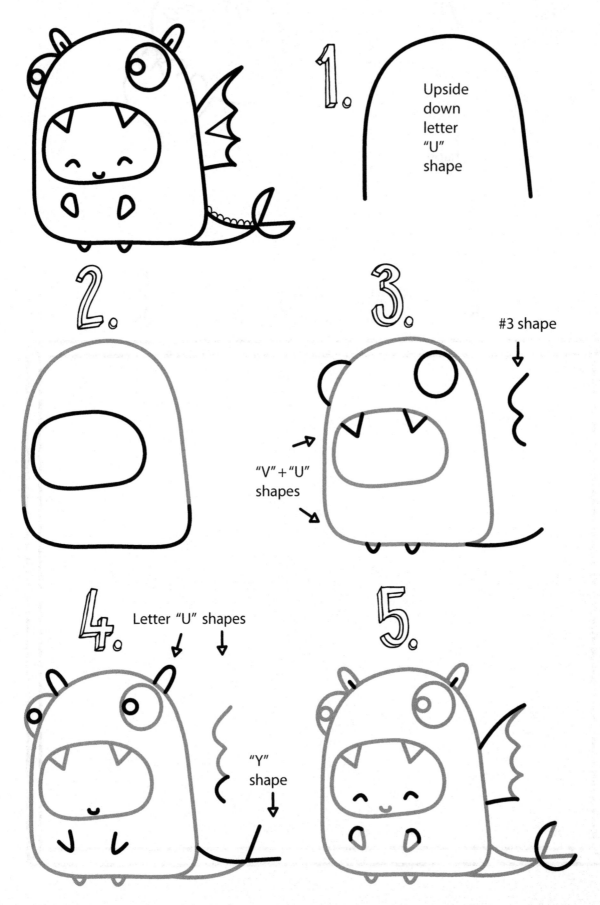

1. Upside down letter "U" shape

2.

3. #3 shape

"V" + "U" shapes

4. Letter "U" shapes

"Y" shape

5.

6.

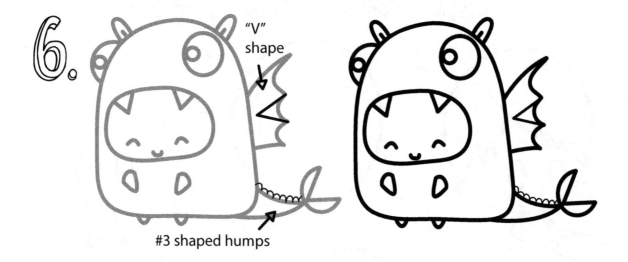

"V" shape

#3 shaped humps

NOW YOU TRY

BEAR AND HIS BOY

1.

2.

Letter "w" shape

3.

Letters "M" + "C" shapes

4.

Letters "c" + "w" shapes

5.

#3 shaped hands

Erase on dotted line

6.

"Y" + "J" + "C" shapes

7.

Erase on dotted lines

NOW YOU TRY

CAT AND HER KITTEN

1.
Draw letters "L" + "M"

2.

3.

4.
Draw a letter "D" + sideways #3 shapes

5.

6.

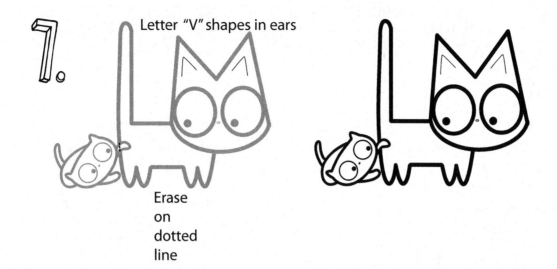

7.

Letter "V" shapes in ears

Erase
on
dotted
line

NOW YOU TRY

FOX AND THE CUTE BALLOON

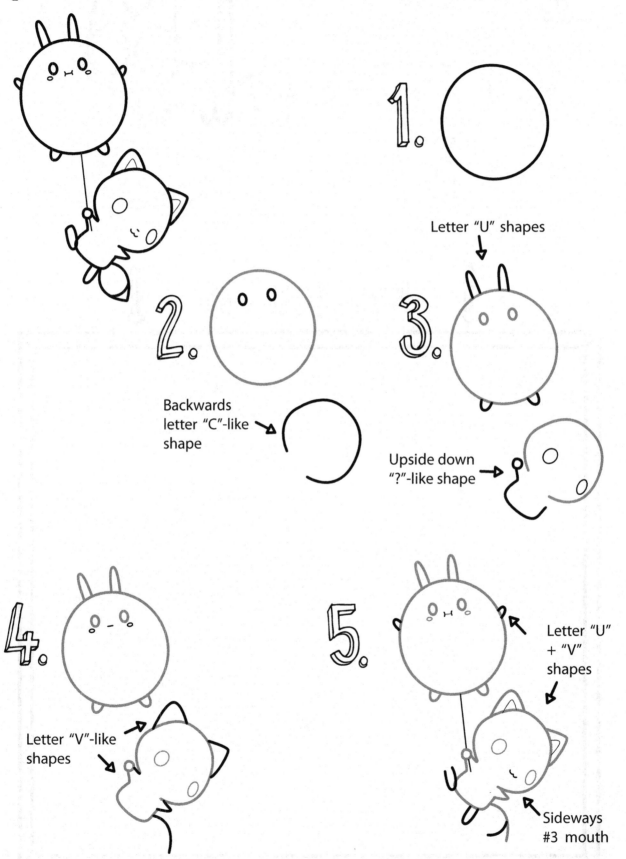

1.

2. Backwards letter "C"-like shape

3. Letter "U" shapes

Upside down "?"-like shape

4. Letter "V"-like shapes

5. Letter "U" + "V" shapes

Sideways #3 mouth

NOW YOU TRY

BEAR IN BUNNY COSTUME

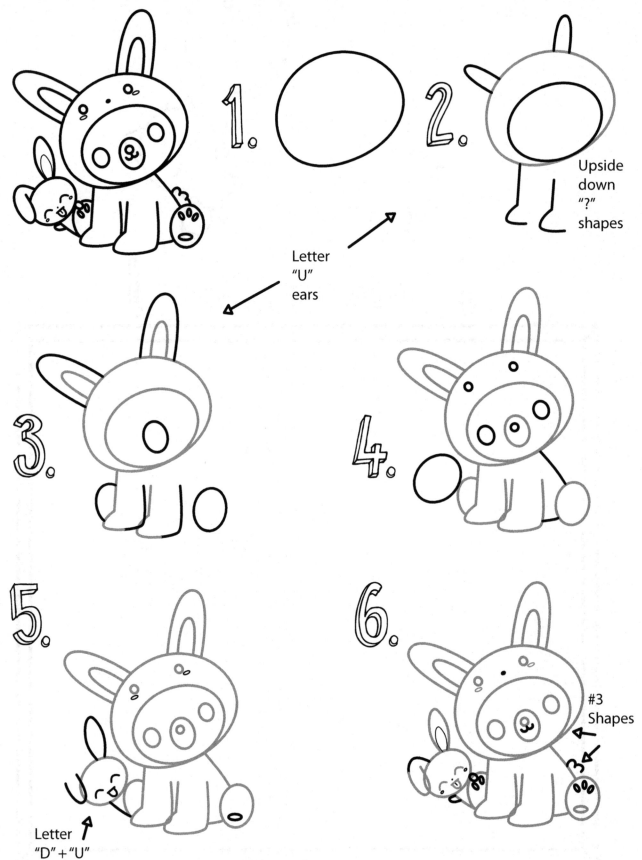

1.

2. Upside down "?" shapes

Letter "U" ears

3.

4.

5. Letter "D" + "U"

6. #3 Shapes

7.

Erase on dotted lines

NOW YOU TRY

HEDGEHOG WITH FLOWER

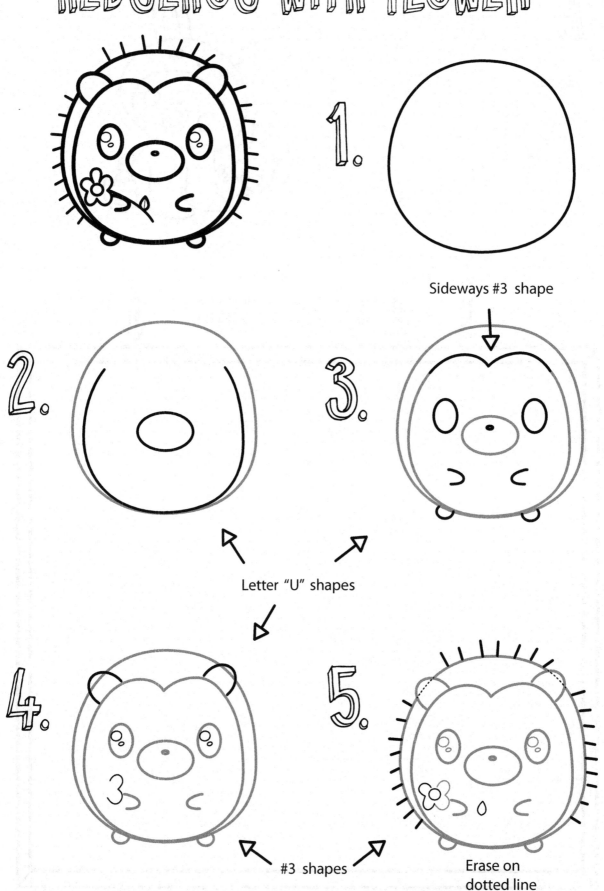

1.

Sideways #3 shape

2.

3.

Letter "U" shapes

4.

5.

#3 shapes

Erase on dotted line

6.

NOW YOU TRY

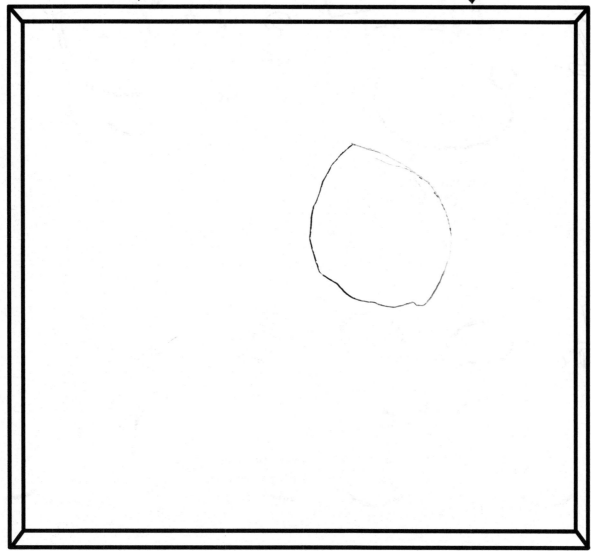

BUNNY RIDING RUBBER DUCKY

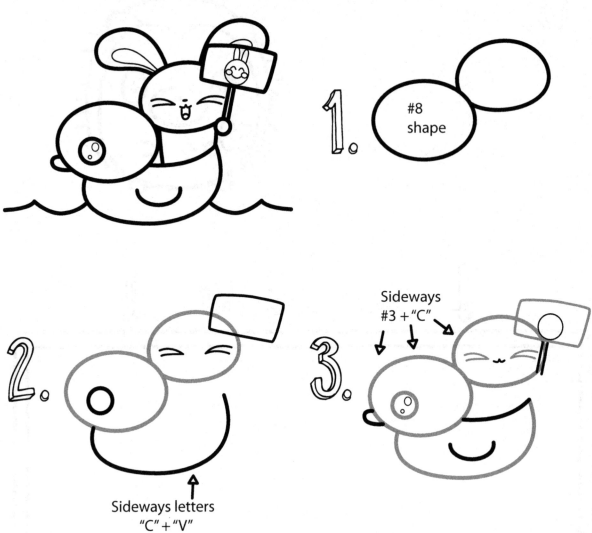

1.

#8 shape

2.

Sideways letters "C" + "V"

3.

Sideways #3 + "C"

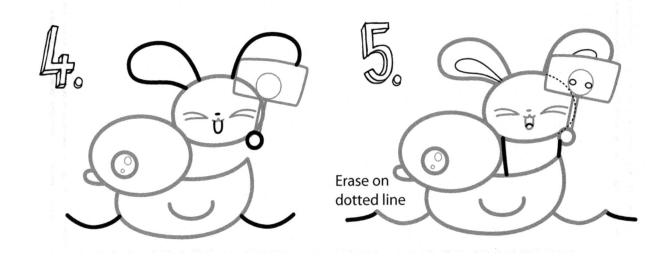

4.

5.

Erase on dotted line

6.

Letter "U"
ears

NOW YOU TRY

DOGGY LOVES HIS HAMSTER

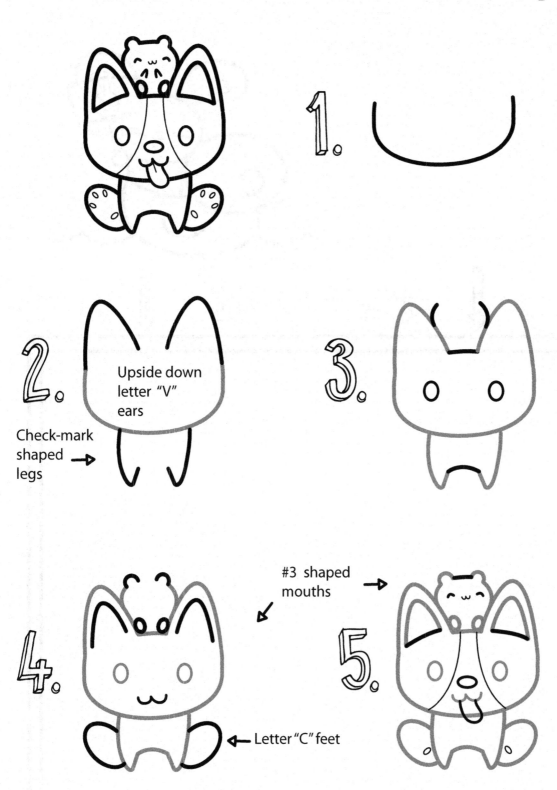

1.

2. Upside down letter "V" ears

Check-mark shaped legs →

3.

4. Letter "C" feet ←

#3 shaped mouths →

5.

6.

Erase
on
dotted
line

NOW YOU TRY

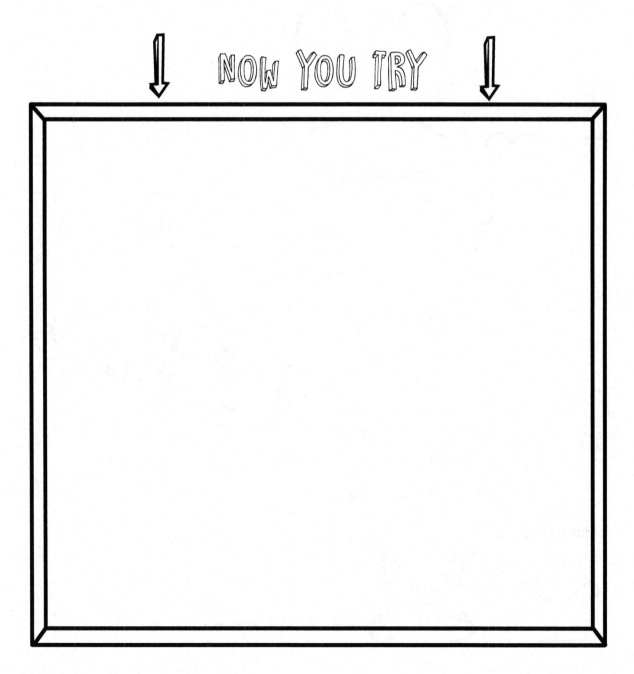

KID IN FROG COSTUME WITH FROG

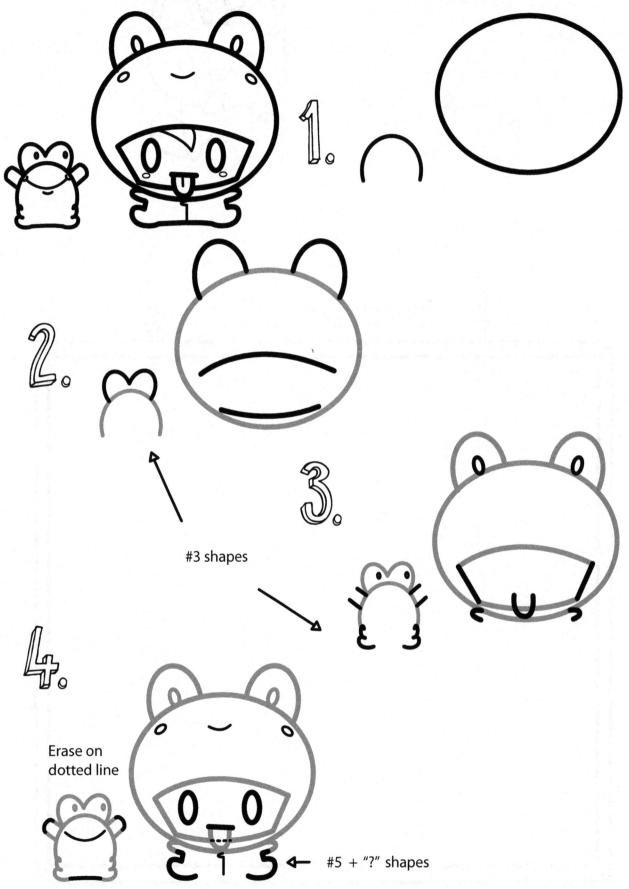

1.

2.

#3 shapes

3.

4.

Erase on
dotted line

#5 + "?" shapes

Letter "V" bangs

NOW YOU TRY

RACCOON DREAMING ABOUT PIZZA

1.

2.

3. Letter "V"-like shapes

4. Letter "V"-like shapes

Erase the dotted lines

5.

#3
shape

NOW YOU TRY

OWL AND BAT BUDDIES

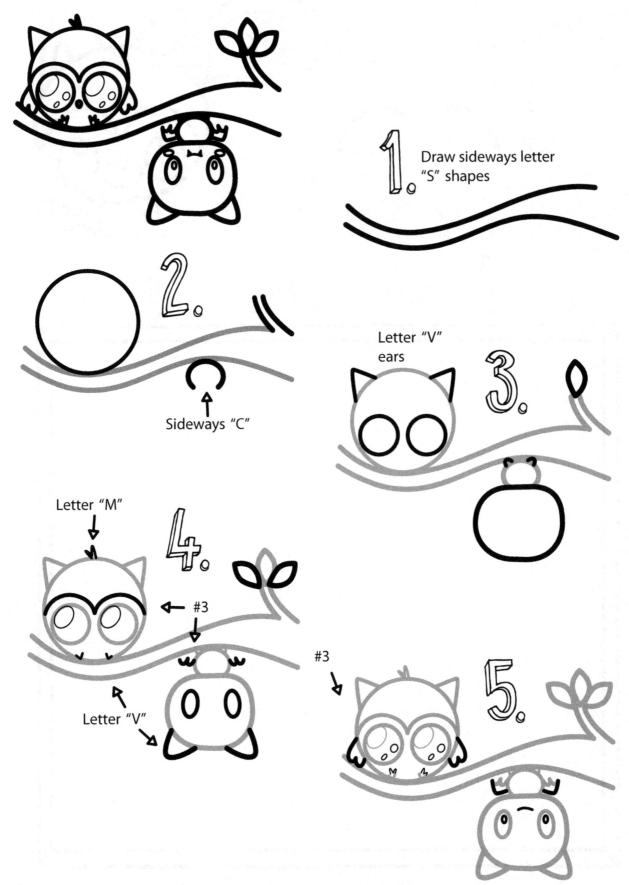

1. Draw sideways letter "S" shapes

2. Sideways "C"

Letter "V" ears

3.

Letter "M"

4. #3

Letter "V"

#3

5.

6.

"U" + "V"

NOW YOU TRY

DOGGY BUTT

1.

2. #7-like ears

3. #3-like shapes

Erase on dotted line

4. Letter "J" shapes

5. "?"-like shape

6.

Erase
on
dotted
line

Letter "X"
shape

NOW YOU TRY

KITTY LOVES FISHY

1.

2.

3. "V" Ears

4. #3 & "e" shapes

5. "U" shaped body
Sideways "D"

6. #3 shape

7.

Erase on dotted lines

Backwards "?"-like shape →

NOW YOU TRY

KID IN UNICORN COSTUME EATS GUMMY BEAR

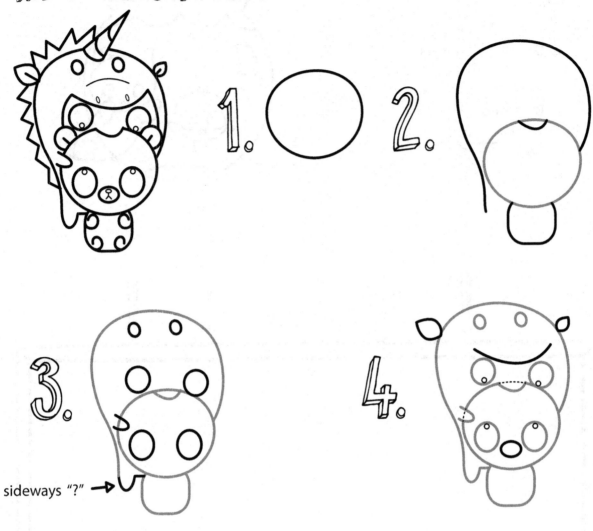

1.

2.

3. sideways "?"

4. Don't draw the dotted lines

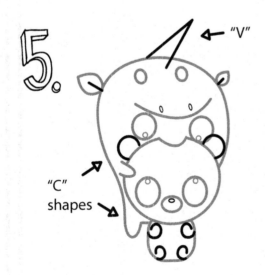

5. "V"

"C" shapes

6. "Y" mouth

7.

NOW YOU TRY

PIG CUPCAKE

1.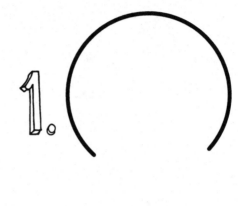

2.

3.

Draw sideways "C" shapes

4. Upside down "?" shapes

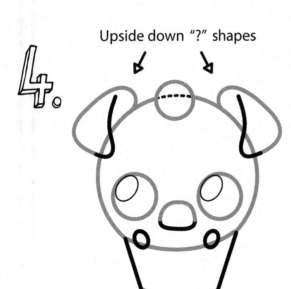

5. Erase on dotted lines

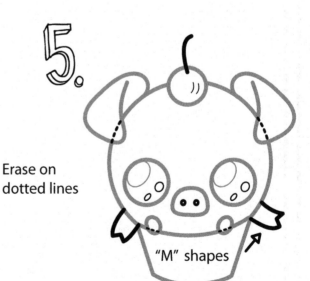

"M" shapes

6.

NOW YOU TRY

SEAL CONE

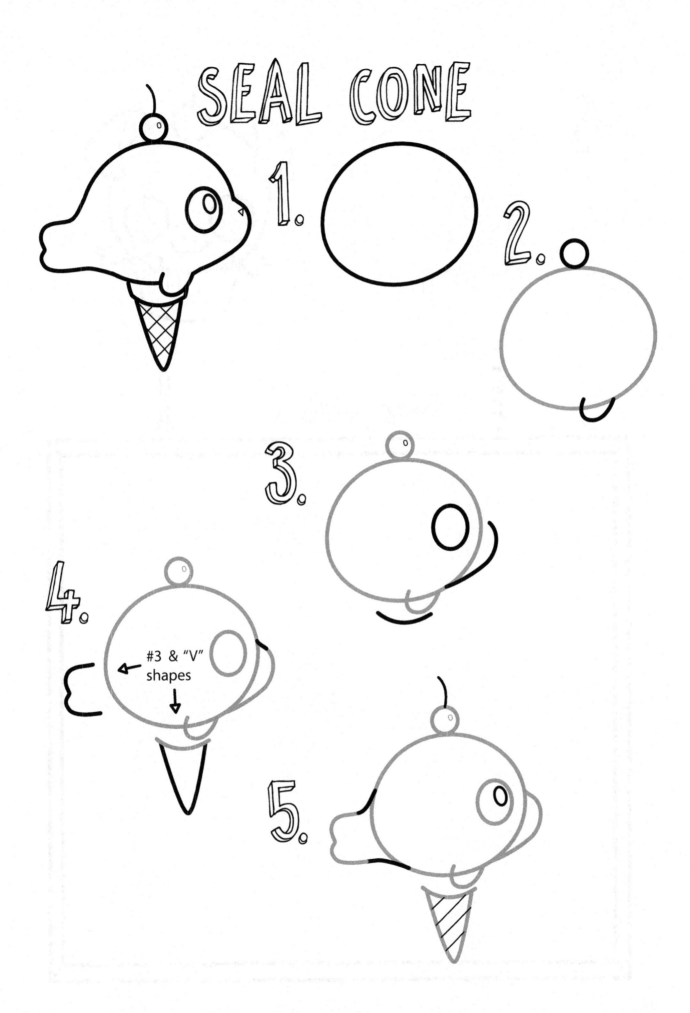

1.

2.

3.

4. #3 & "V" shapes

5.

6.

Erase the
dotted lines

NOW YOU TRY

TURTLE DONUT

1.

2.

3.

4. Erase on dotted line

5. Draw wavy line along bottom of the donut

Sideways #3 shapes

6.

NOW YOU TRY

MONSTER BUDDIES

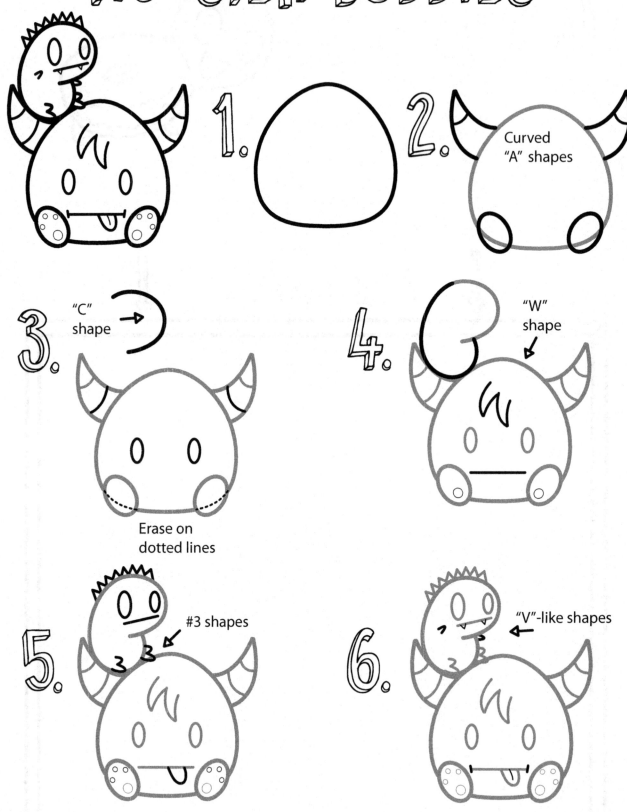

1.

2. Curved "A" shapes

3. "C" shape →
Erase on dotted lines

4. "W" shape

5. #3 shapes
3 3

6. "V"-like shapes

7.

Erase
on
dotted
line

NOW YOU TRY

SHARK COSTUME

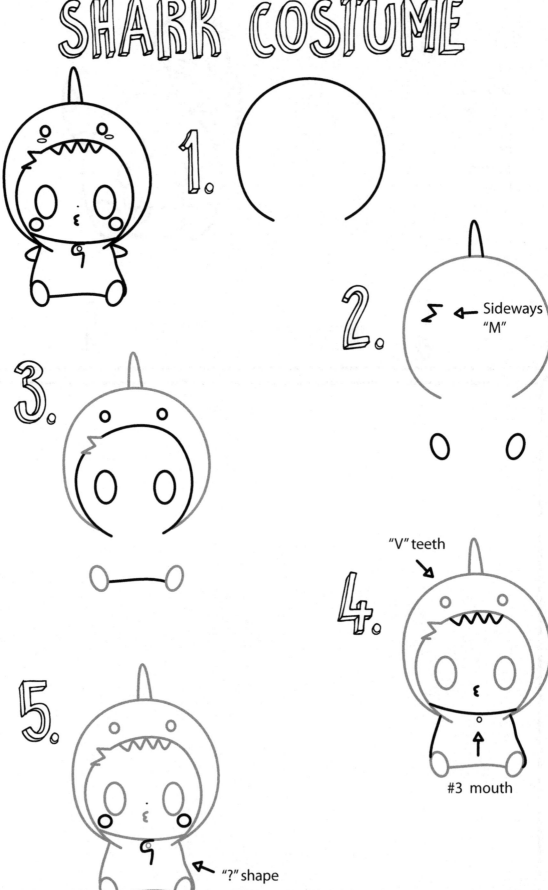

1.

2. Sideways "M"

3.

4. "V" teeth

#3 mouth

5. "?" shape

6.

NOW YOU TRY

CUTESY PLATYPUS

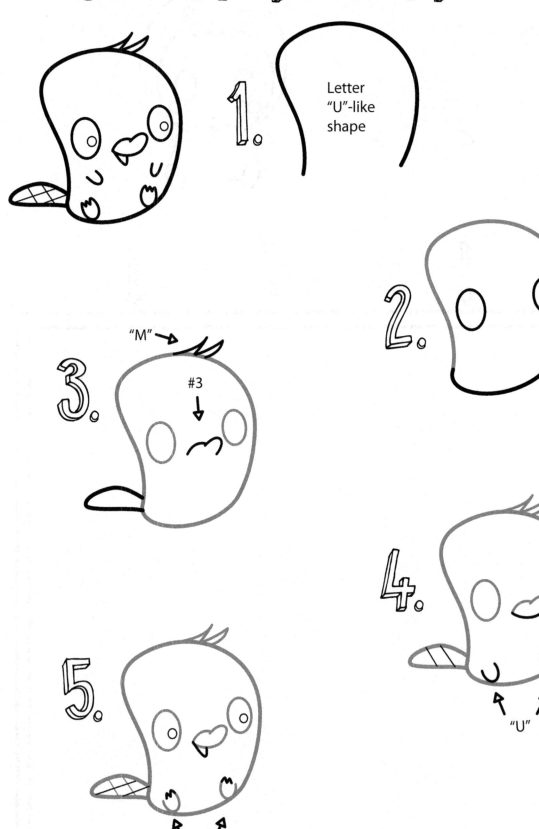

1. Letter "U"-like shape

2.

3. "M"
#3

4. "U"

5. "M"

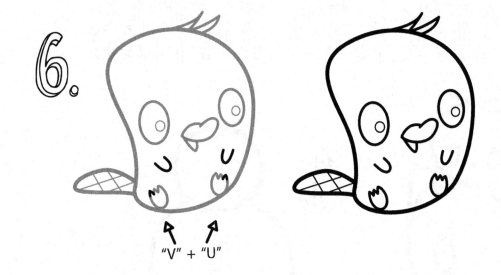

6.

"V" + "U"

NOW YOU TRY

STACKED KITTIES

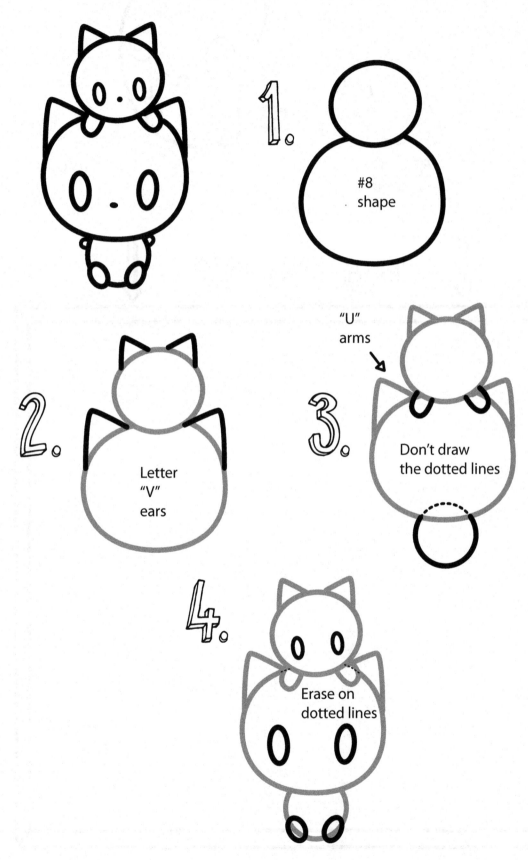

1.

#8
shape

2.

Letter
"V"
ears

3.

"U"
arms

Don't draw
the dotted lines

4.

Erase on
dotted lines

5.

Erase the
dotted lines

NOW YOU TRY

FISH SPITTING ON BIRD

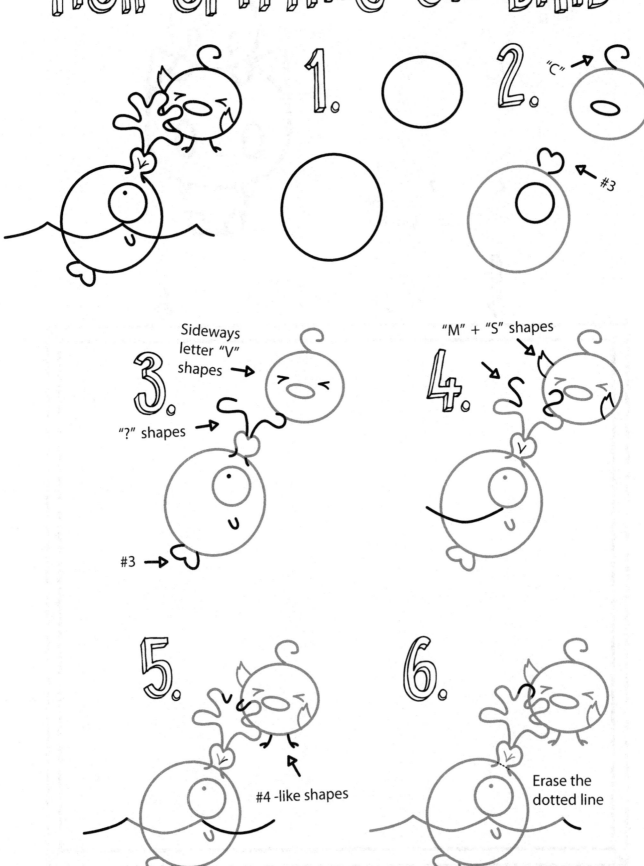

1.

2. "C" →

#3

3. Sideways letter "V" shapes →

"?" shapes →

#3 →

4. "M" + "S" shapes

5. #4 -like shapes

6. Erase the dotted line

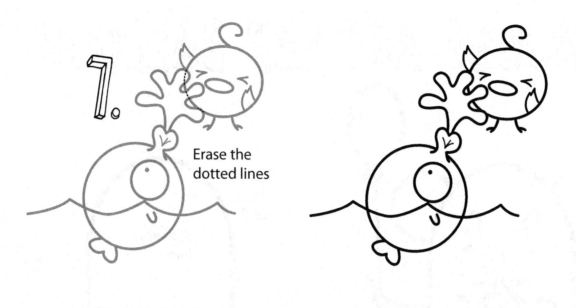

7. Erase the
dotted lines

NOW YOU TRY

MOUSE AND HER BALLOON

1. Sideways letter "D"

2.

3.

4.

5. Erase the dotted lines

6.

NOW YOU TRY

CUTESY TIGER

1.

2.

Don't draw the dotted lines

3.

#3 shapes

Letter "V" shapes

4.

5.

6. Letter "U" arms

7. Erase on dotted line

NOW YOU TRY

SEAL WITH PENGUIN BALL

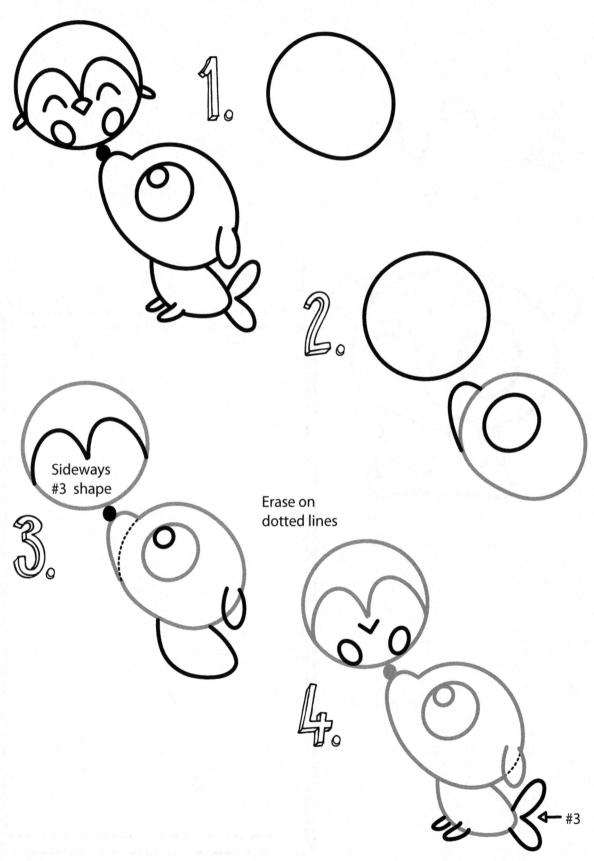

1.

2.

3. Sideways #3 shape

Erase on dotted lines

4. #3

5.

Erase on dotted line

NOW YOU TRY

TURTLE EATING PIZZA

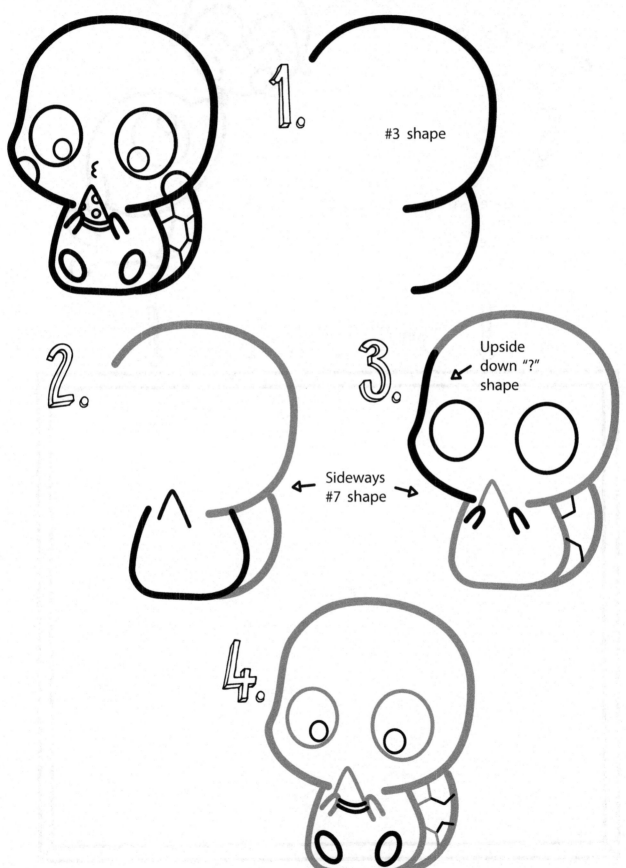

1.

#3 shape

2.

Sideways #7 shape

3.

Upside down "?" shape

4.

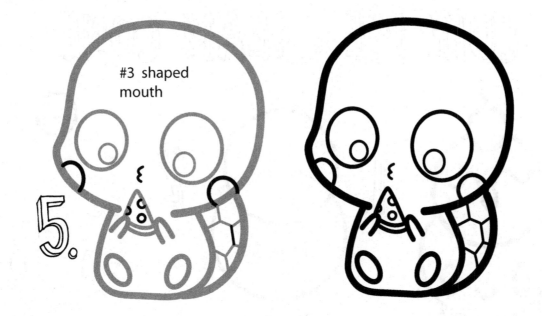

#3 shaped mouth

5.

NOW YOU TRY

CUTE ICE CREAM CONE

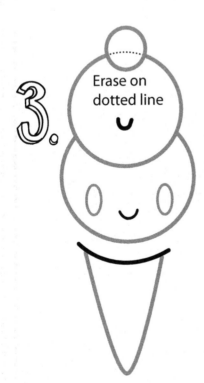

1.

#8 shape

Don't draw
the dotted lines

2.

"V"
shape

3.

Erase on
dotted line

Sideways
#3 shapes

4.

NOW YOU TRY

CUTE FRENCH FRIES

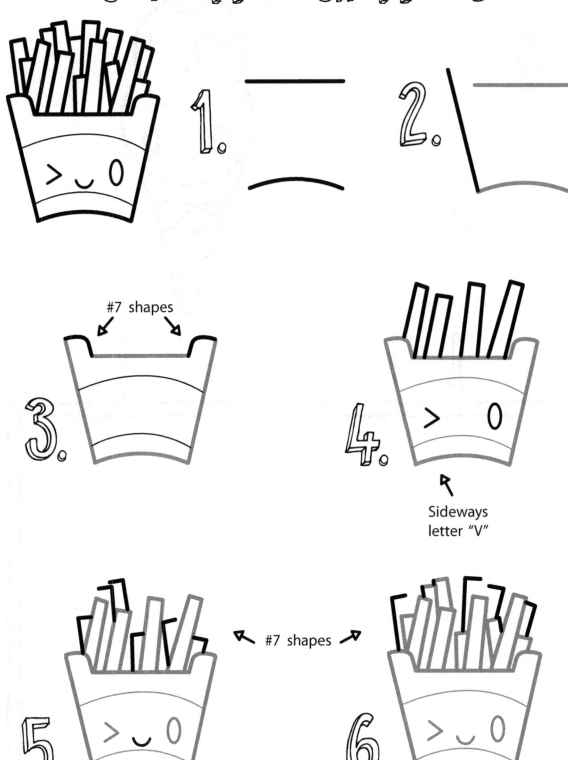

1.

2.

3. #7 shapes

4. Sideways letter "V"

5. #7 shapes

6.

7.

NOW YOU TRY

DOG IN SHARK HAT

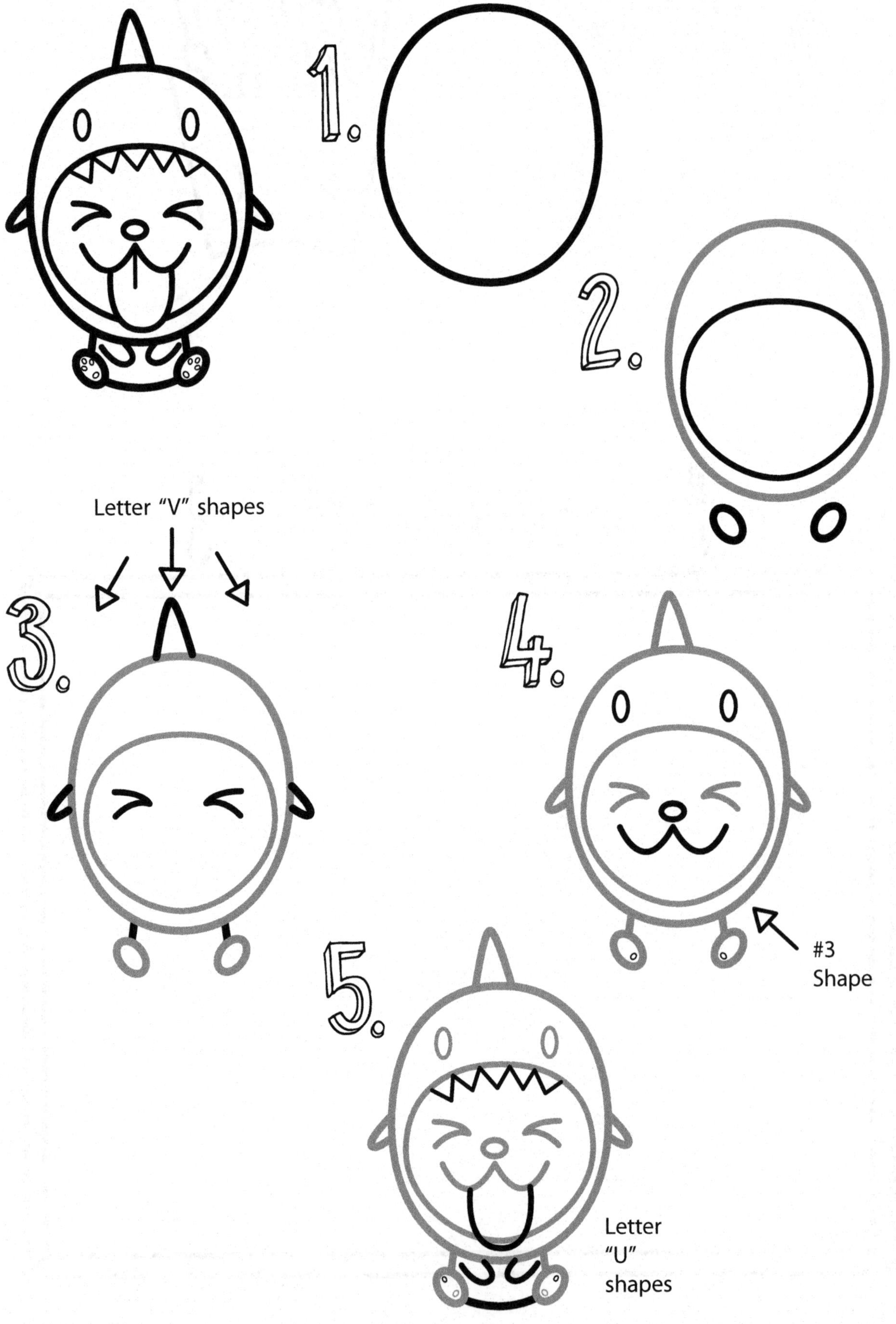

1.

2.

Letter "V" shapes

3.

4.

#3 Shape

5.

Letter "U" shapes

6.

Erase
on
dotted
lines

NOW YOU TRY

EATING A LOLLIPOP

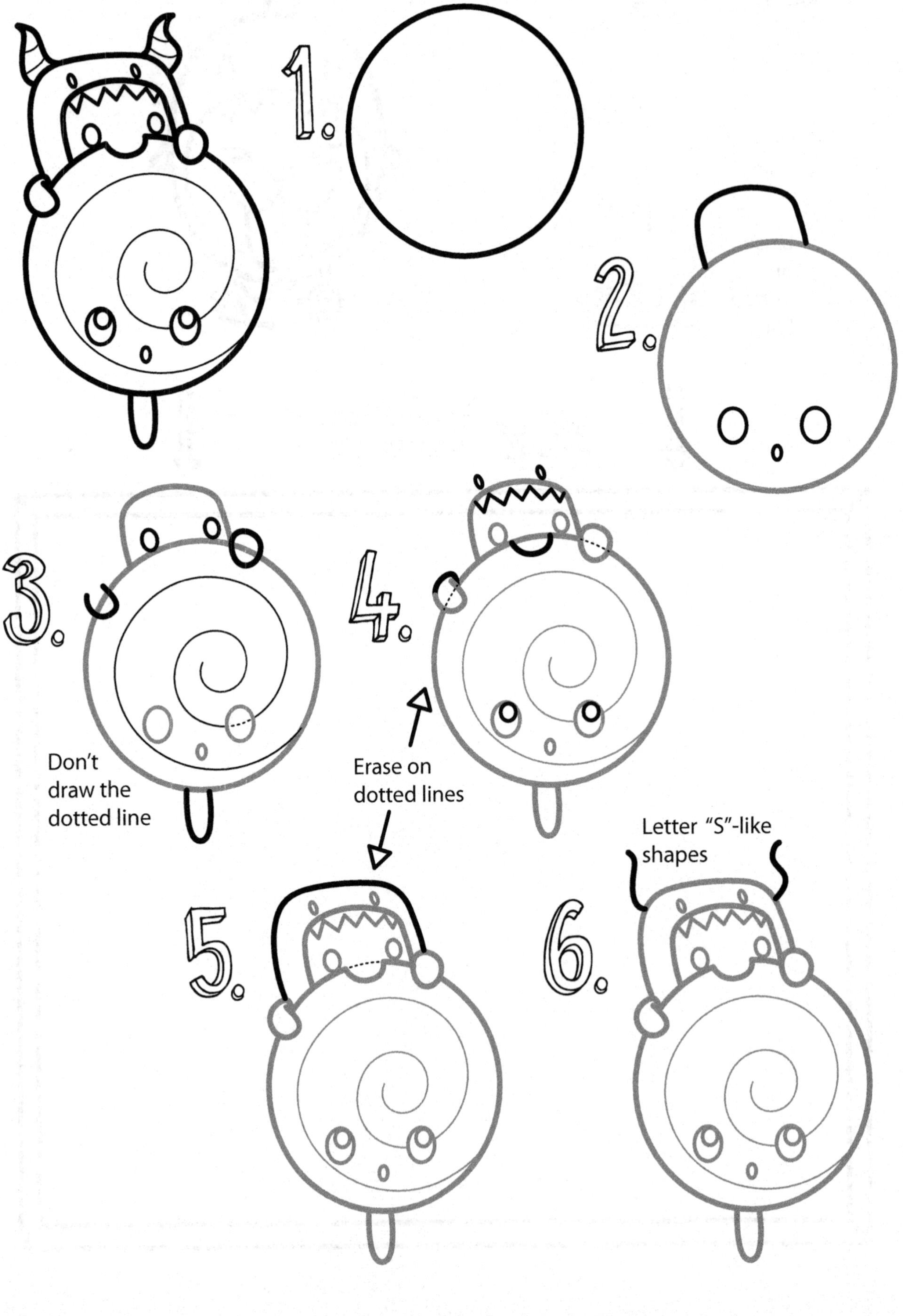

1.

2.

3.

Don't draw the dotted line

4.

Erase on dotted lines

5.

6.

Letter "S"-like shapes

7.

Letter "S"-like curves

8.

↓ NOW YOU TRY ↓

KITTY HUGS

"C" shape

1.

Letter "V" shapes

2.

Upside down "?" shape

Sideways #3 shape

Letter "V" shapes

3.

4.

5.

Letter "U" + "V" shapes

6.

Sideways "?" + "C" shapes

7.

#3 shapes

↓ NOW YOU TRY ↓

RACCOON AND MONKEY BALLOON

1. Letter "U" shape

2. #3 shapes

3. Letter "C" shapes

Upside down "?" shapes

Letter "M"

4. Erase on dotted line

Sideways #3 + "V" shapes

5. Letter "V" shapes

Upside down "?" shapes

6. Erase on dotted line

Letter "S" shape. Don't draw dotted line.

7.

NOW YOU TRY

BUNNY WANTS ICE CREAM

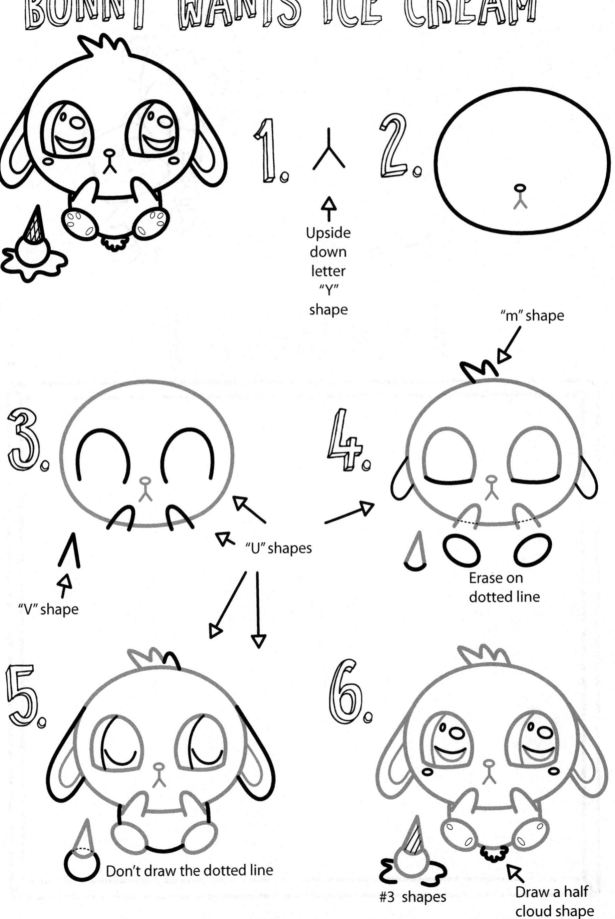

1. Upside down letter "Y" shape

2.

3. "V" shape

"U" shapes

4. Erase on dotted line

"m" shape

5. Don't draw the dotted line

6. #3 shapes

Draw a half cloud shape

7.

Erase on
dotted line

NOW YOU TRY

KITTY IN THE CUP

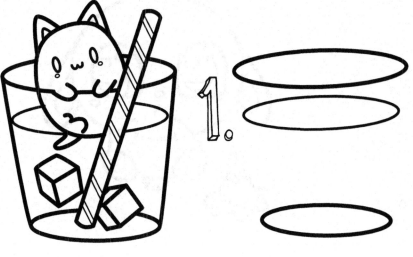

1.

2.

Letter "U" shapes

3.

Erase on dotted lines

"V" ears

4.

#3 shapes

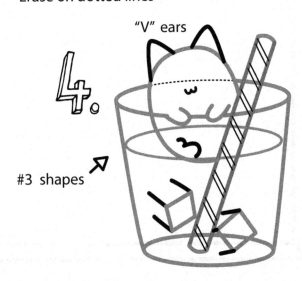

5.

Erase on dotted lines

6.

NOW YOU TRY

DOGGY SUPER HERO

1. Draw an upside down "?" shape

2.

3. Draw a flattened #2 shape

"?" shape

4. #3 shapes

letter "M"-like shape

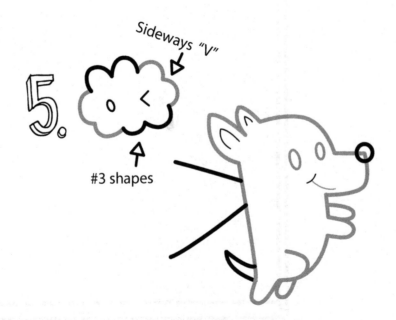

5. Sideways "V"

#3 shapes

6.

Letter "D" mouth

NOW YOU TRY

KID IN A BEAR COSTUME

1. Upside down letter "U" shape

2. Don't draw the dotted lines

3.

4.

5.

6.

NOW YOU TRY

COOL CHICK AND BEE

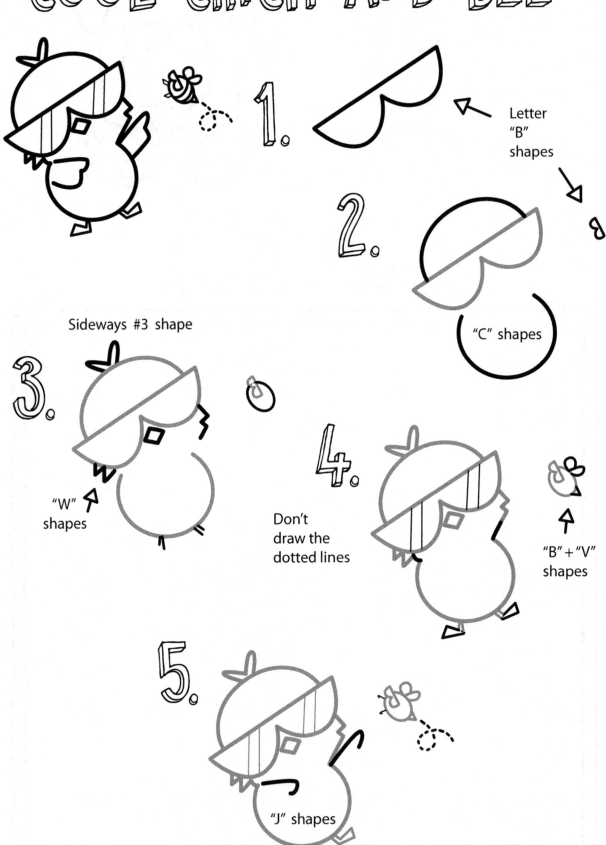

1.

Letter "B" shapes

2.

"C" shapes

Sideways #3 shape

3.

"W" shapes

Don't draw the dotted lines

4.

"B" + "V" shapes

5.

"J" shapes

6.

NOW YOU TRY

FANCY ELEPHANT

1. "Q" shape

2.

3. Erase on dotted lines

#3

Upside down #7 shape

4. Don't draw the dotted lines

5.

6.

NOW YOU TRY

FOX AND A KITE

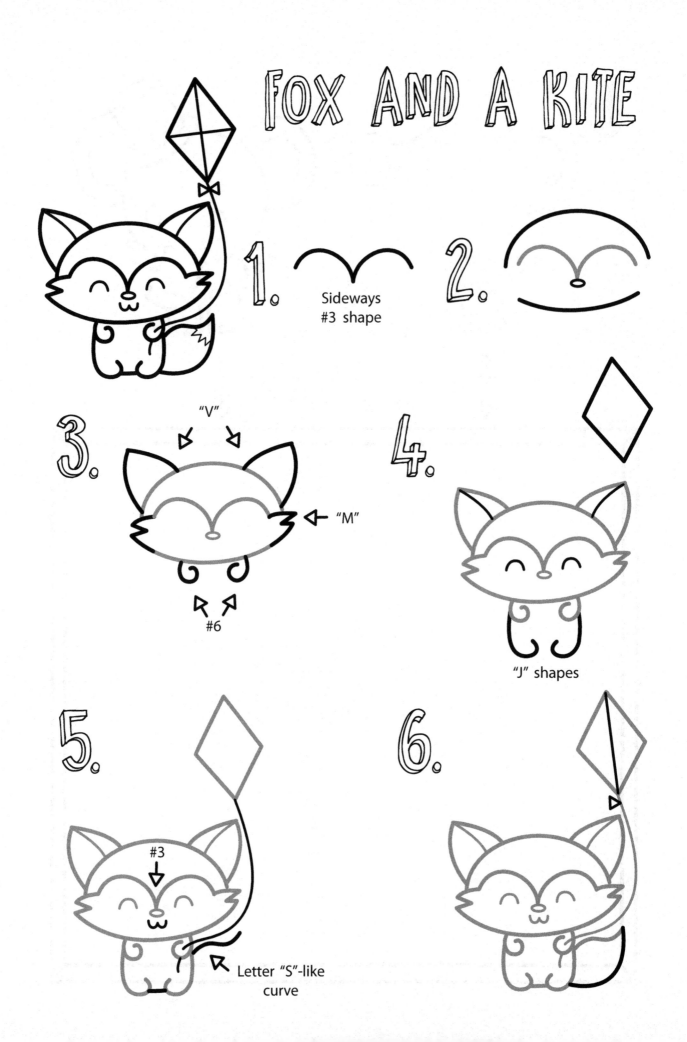

1. Sideways #3 shape

2.

3. "V"
"M"
#6

4. "J" shapes

5. #3
Letter "S"-like curve

6.

7.

NOW YOU TRY

DOG IN FROG COSTUME WITH FROG

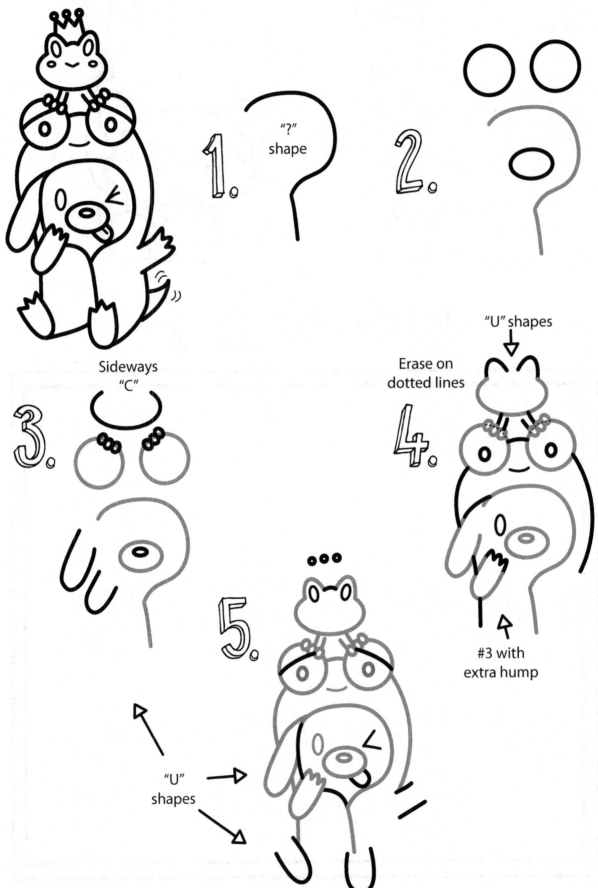

1. "?" shape

2.

3. Sideways "C"

4. Erase on dotted lines — "U" shapes
#3 with extra hump

5. "U" shapes

6.

"M" + "W" shapes

7.

"V"

"V"

NOW YOU TRY

SNAIL AND HER MUG

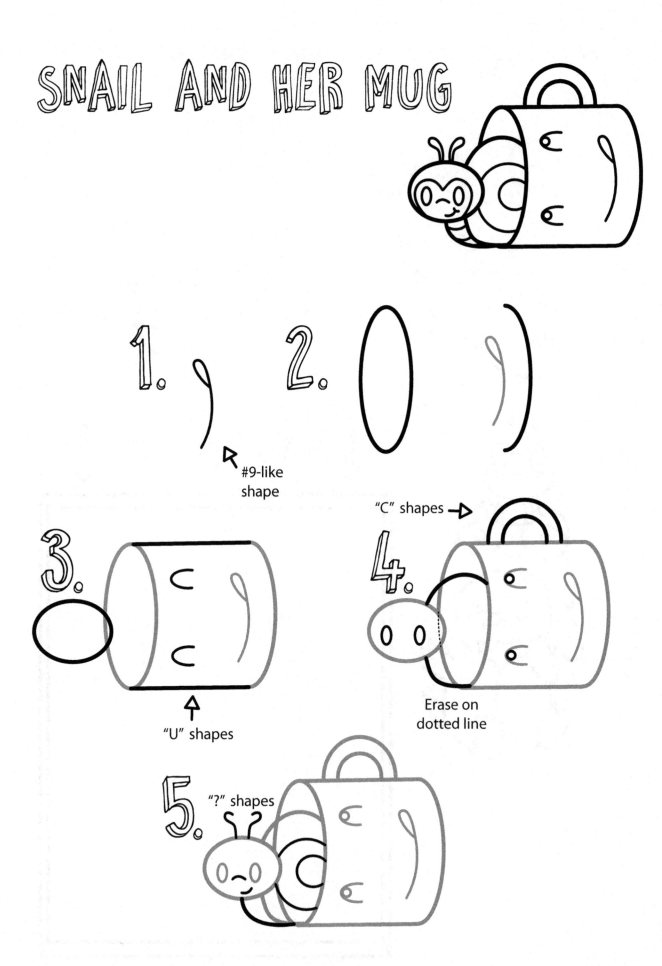

1.

#9-like shape

2.

3.

"U" shapes

"C" shapes →

4.

Erase on dotted line

5.

"?" shapes

Sideways #3 shape

Erase on dotted lines

NOW YOU TRY

BUNNIES KISSING

1.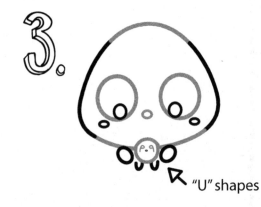

2. 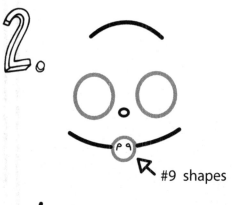 #9 shapes

3. "U" shapes

4. 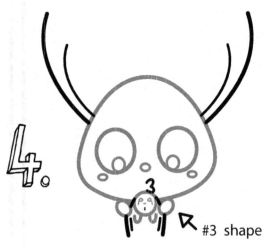 #3 shape

5.  "J" shapes

6.

#3 shaped legs

NOW YOU TRY

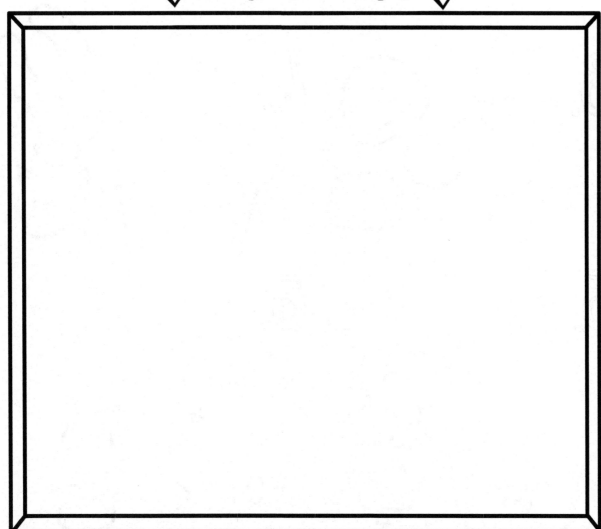

YUMMY CUPCAKE

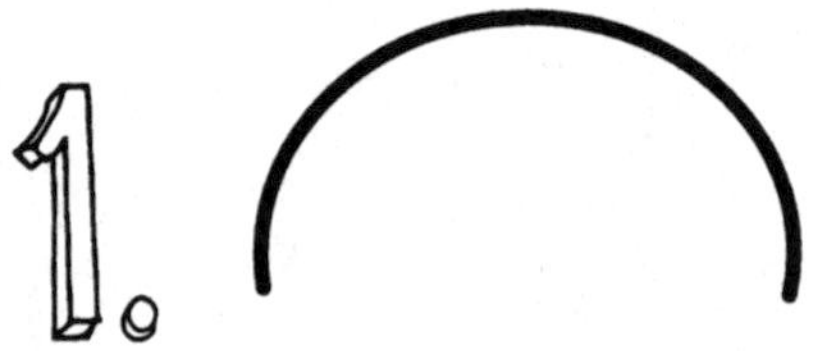

1.

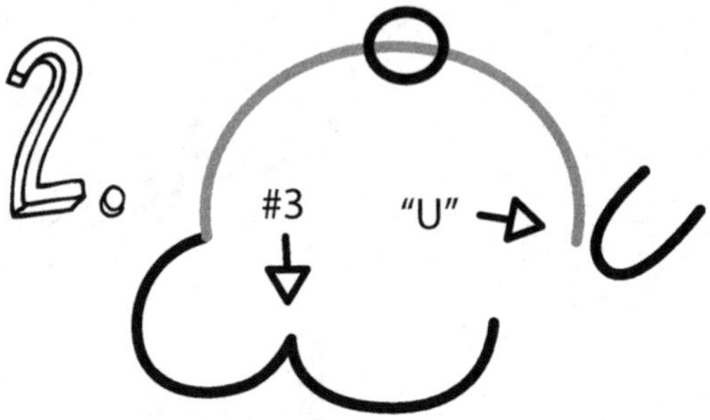

2. #3 "U"

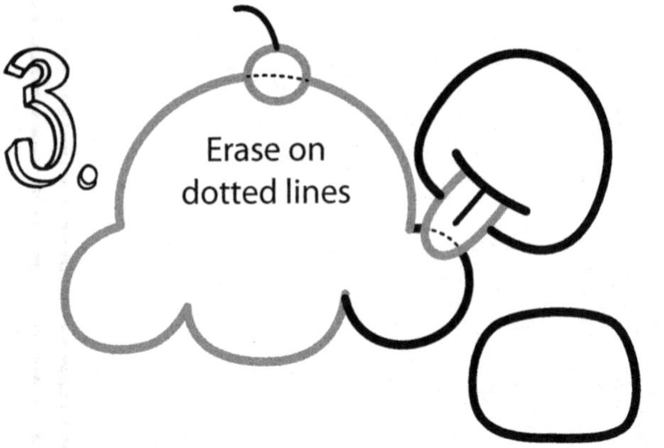

3. Erase on dotted lines

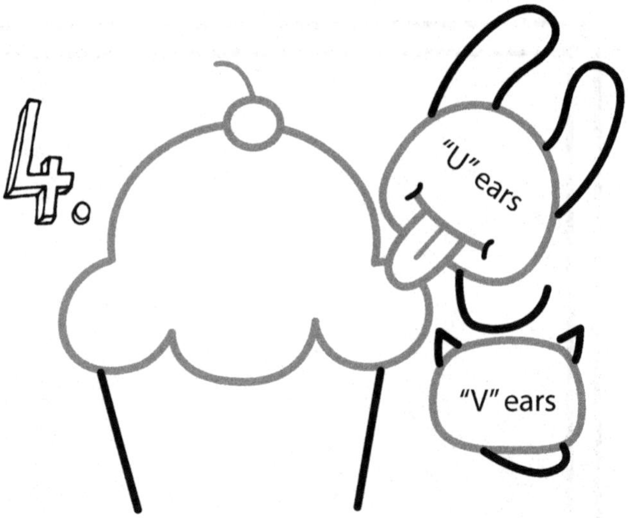

4. "U" ears   "V" ears

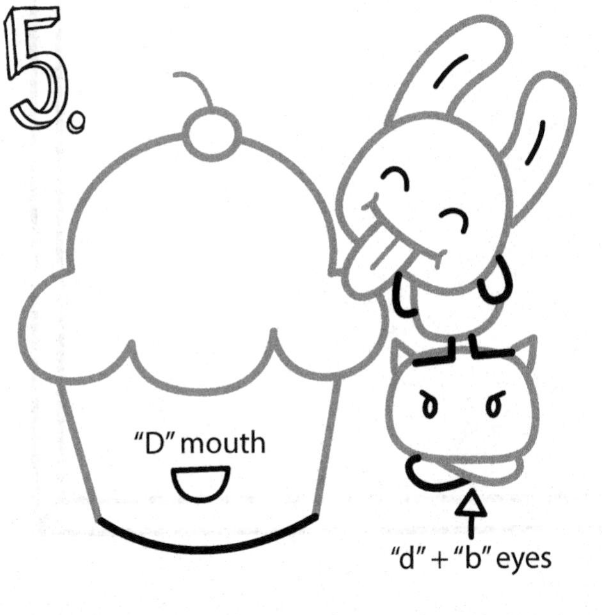

5. "D" mouth   "d" + "b" eyes

6. sideways "V"

7.

Erase on dotted lines

8.

Don't draw dotted lines

NOW YOU TRY

BUMBLY BEE

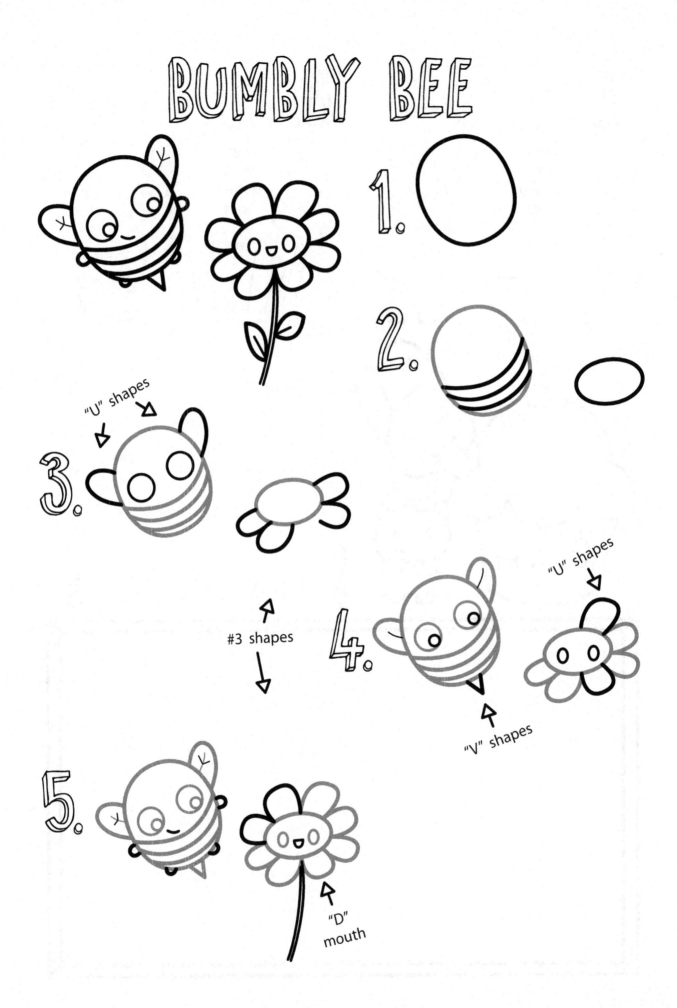

1.

2.

3. "U" shapes

#3 shapes

4. "U" shapes

"V" shapes

5. "D" mouth

6.

7.

NOW YOU TRY

JUMPY UNICORN

1. #C shape

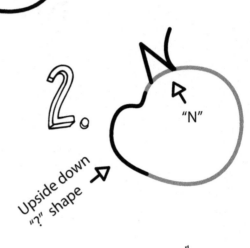

2. "N"

Upside down "?" shape

3. "S"-like curve

"V"

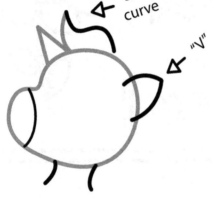

4. "s" curves

"F" shapes

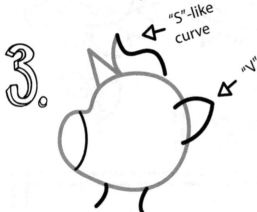

5. Erase on the dotted line

#5 + #3 shapes

"?"-like shape

6.

⬇ NOW YOU TRY ⬇

TACO CAT AND FRIENDS

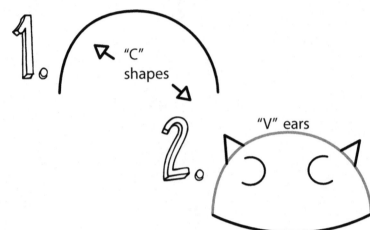

1. "C" shapes

2. "V" ears

3. "U" shapes

4. "C" shape
#3

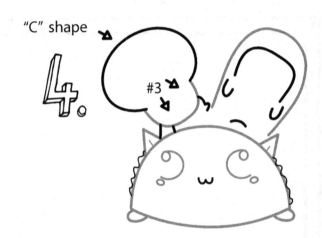

5. "C" ears

6.

7.

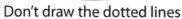

Don't draw the dotted lines

↓ NOW YOU TRY ↓

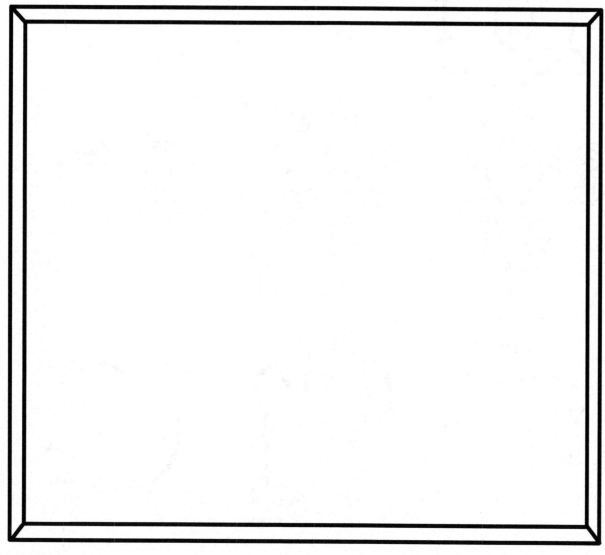

BALANCING ACT

1.

"?" Shapes

2.

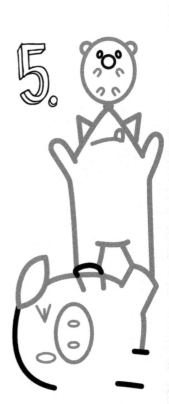

3.

"V" shapes

#9 shape

4.

"C" + "U" shapes

blockish "?" shape

5.

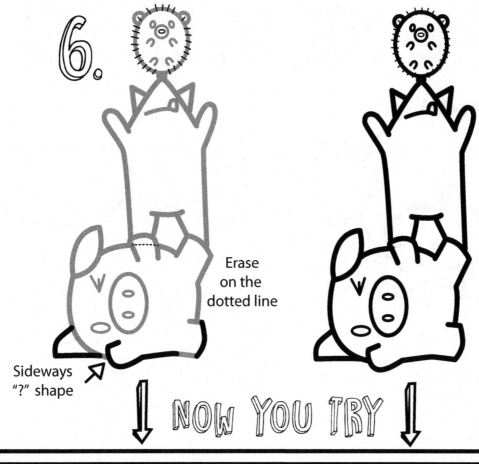

6.

Erase
on the
dotted line

Sideways
"?" shape

NOW YOU TRY

TONGUE OUT SILLY GIRL

1. Letter "P"

2. Sideways "V" shapes

3. "V" + "M" shapes

4. "W" + "V" + "C" shapes

5. "S"

"?" shapes

#3 shapes

6.

Erase on the dotted lines

NOW YOU TRY

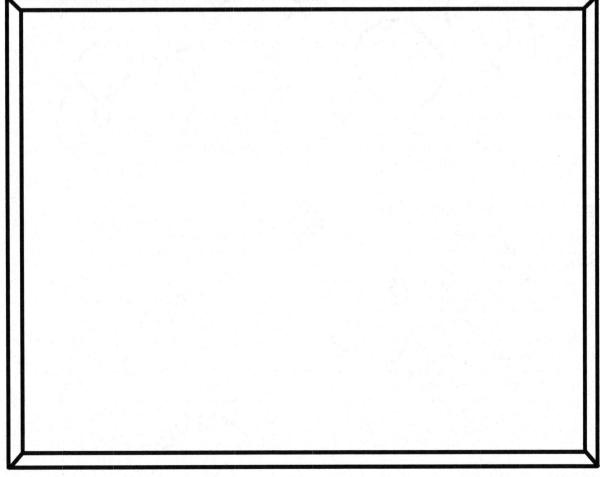

DON'T EAT THE DONUT COSTUME

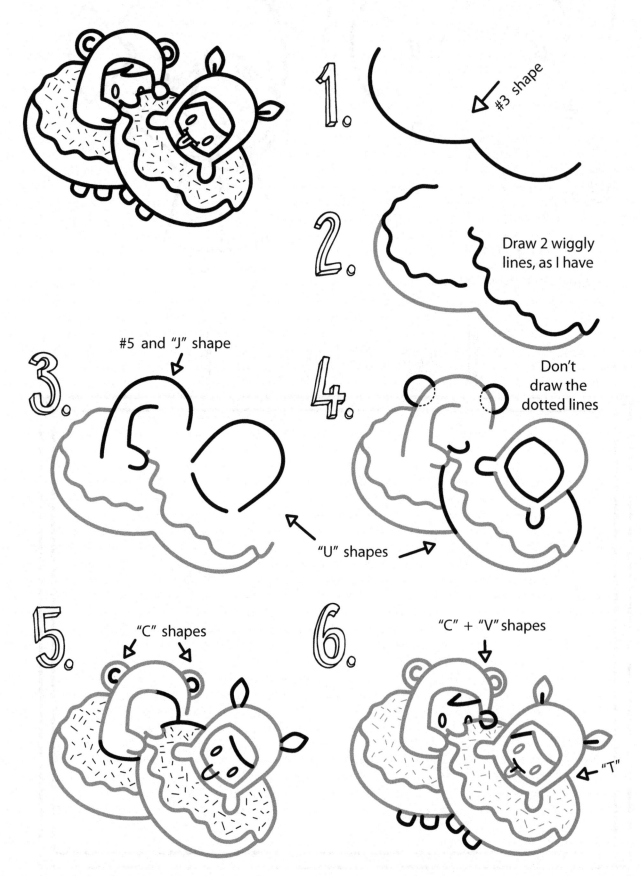

1. #3 shape

2. Draw 2 wiggly lines, as I have

3. #5 and "J" shape

4. Don't draw the dotted lines

"U" shapes

5. "C" shapes

6. "C" + "V" shapes

"T"

7.

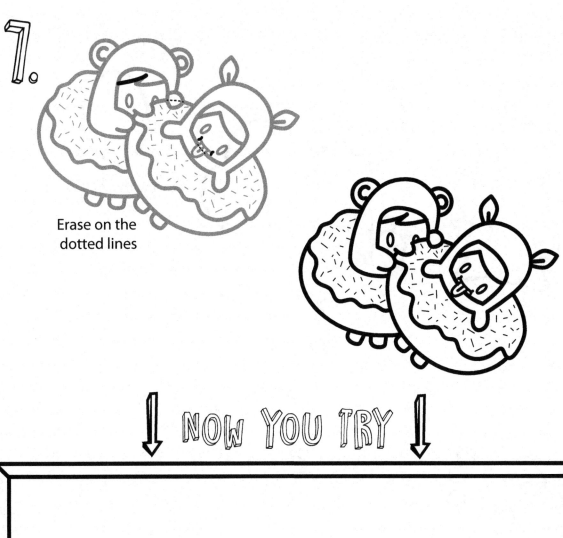

Erase on the
dotted lines

↓ NOW YOU TRY ↓

HIPPO AND THE MOUSE'S BALLOON

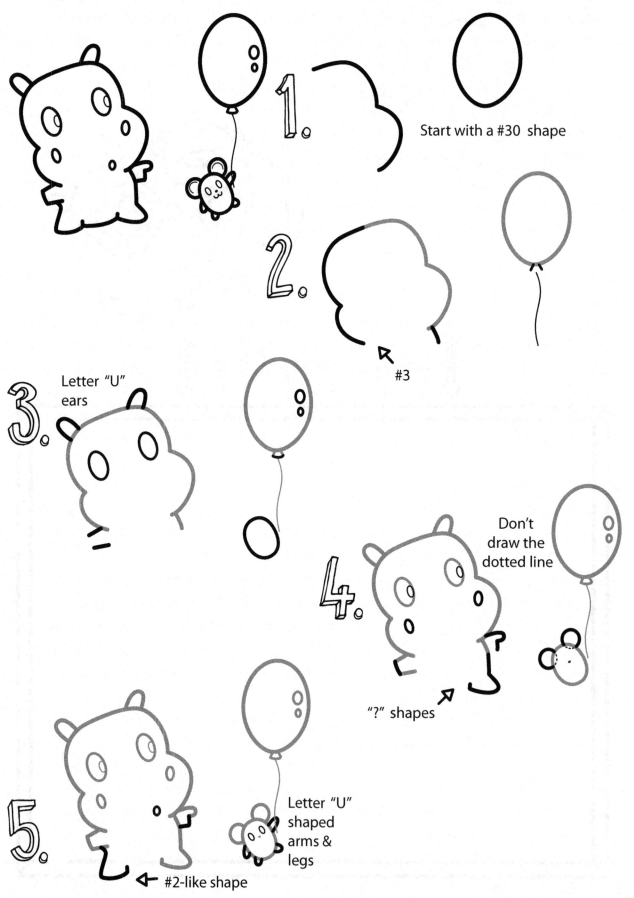

1. Start with a #30 shape

2. #3

3. Letter "U" ears

4. "?" shapes

Don't draw the dotted line

5. Letter "U" shaped arms & legs

#2-like shape

6.

#3

NOW YOU TRY

BUNNY LOVES GIFTS

1. Upside down "U" shape

2. Sideways #3 shape

3. Sideways "C" eyes

"U" shapes

4.

5. Sideways "D" mouth

"V" shapes

6.

Don't draw the dotted lines

NOW YOU TRY

KID IN DINO COSTUME

1. #8 Shape

2.

3. Upside down "?" shaped legs

4.

5. Sideways "V"

6.

7.

Sideways
"D" mouth

NOW YOU TRY

NARWHAL ICE CREAM CONE

1.

"V" shape

2.

"V" shape

3.

4.

"S"-like shaped curves

Erase on the dotted lines

5.

6.

NOW YOU TRY

A FISHING PARROT

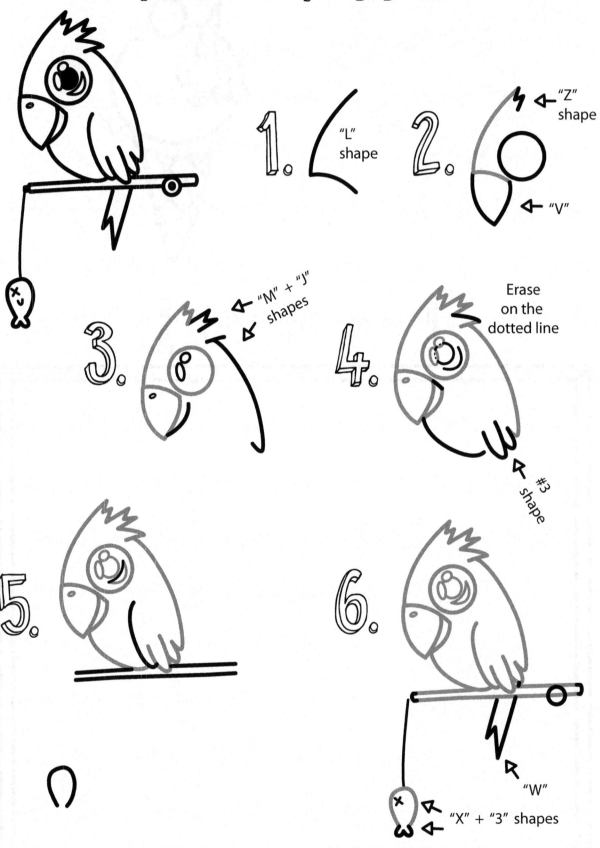

1. "L" shape

2. "Z" shape
"V"

3. "M" + "J" shapes

4. Erase on the dotted line
#3 shape

5.

6. "W"
"X" + "3" shapes

Erase
on the
dotted line

NOW YOU TRY

PENCIL DRAWING FLYING SAUCER

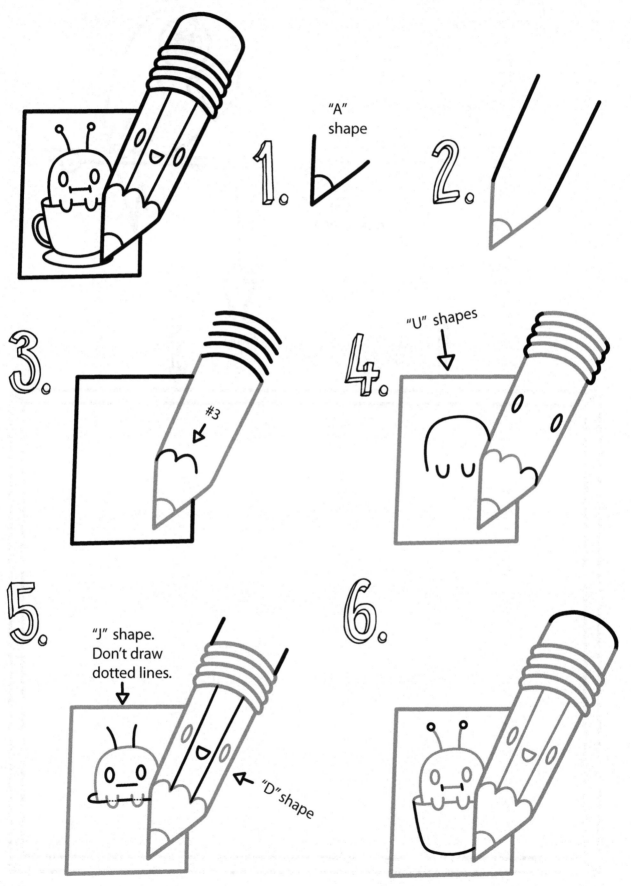

1. "A" shape

2.

3. #3

4. "U" shapes

5. "J" shape. Don't draw dotted lines.   "D" shape

6.

7.

"C"

Don't draw the dotted line

NOW YOU TRY

ANGRY DOG

1. #8-like Shape

2. Sideways "S"-like shape → *(arrow)*

3. "d" + "b" shapes

Don't draw the dotted lines

4. #3 shapes

"V"-shaped ears

Erase the lines that are inside his arms.

5. Erase on the dotted lines

NOW YOU TRY

BABY CHICK ON A BABY EGG

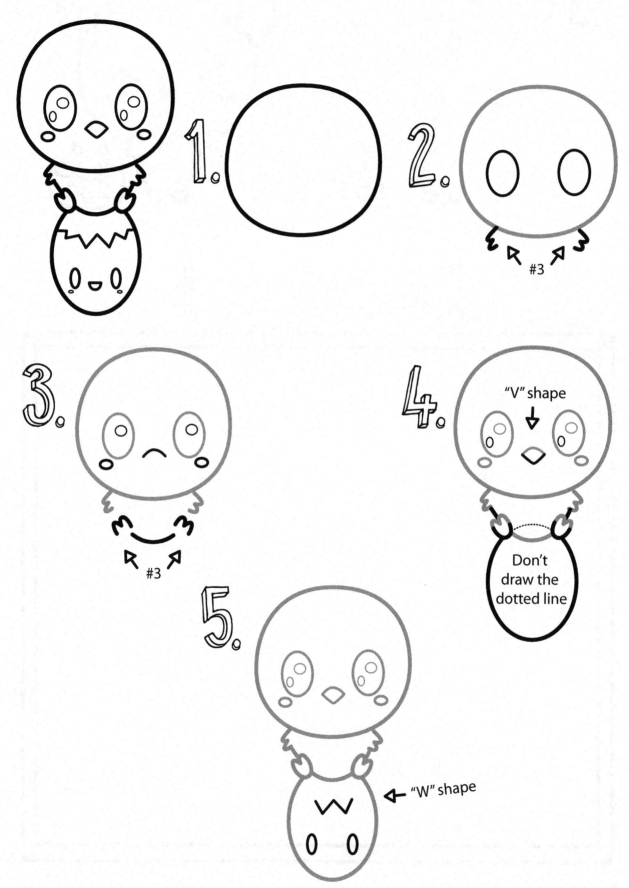

1.

2.
#3

3.
#3

4.
"V" shape
Don't draw the dotted line

5.
"W" shape

6.

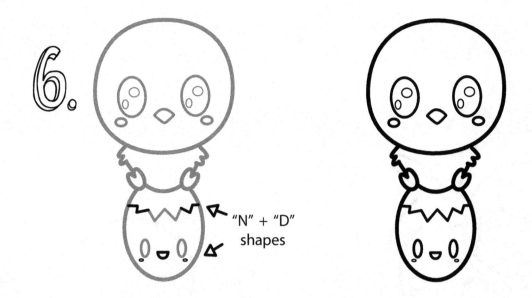

"N" + "D" shapes

NOW YOU TRY

KID IN BUNNY COSTUME WITH BUNNY

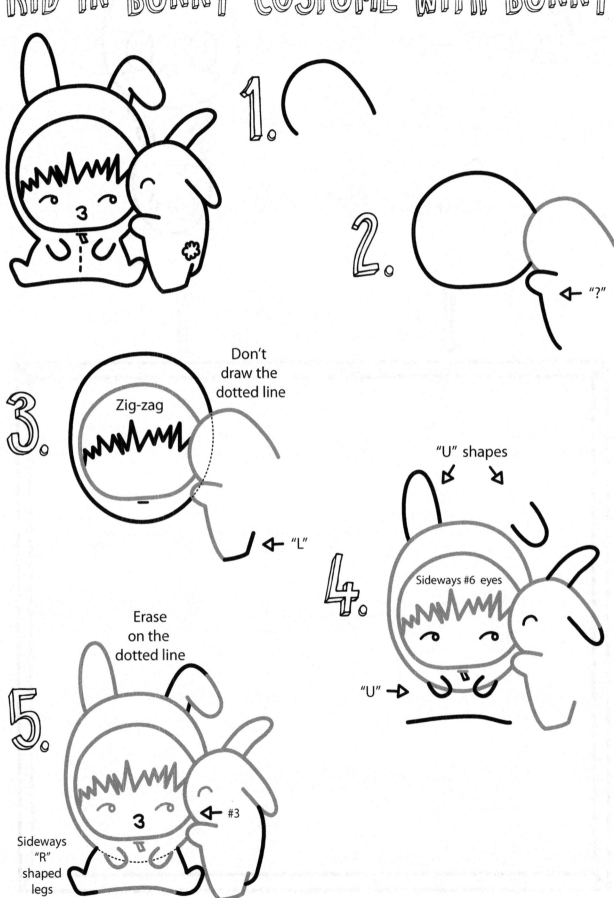

1.

2. ← "?"

3. Zig-zag
Don't draw the dotted line
← "L"

4. "U" shapes
Sideways #6 eyes
"U" →

5. Erase on the dotted line
Sideways "R" shaped legs
← #3

6.

Draw a cloud for the tail.

NOW YOU TRY

HAPPY HOT CHOCOLATE

1. "p" Shape

2. "C" Shape

3.

Erase on the dotted lines

4. Don't draw the dotted line

5.

6. Sideways "V" shape

NOW YOU TRY

RUNNING HAMSTER

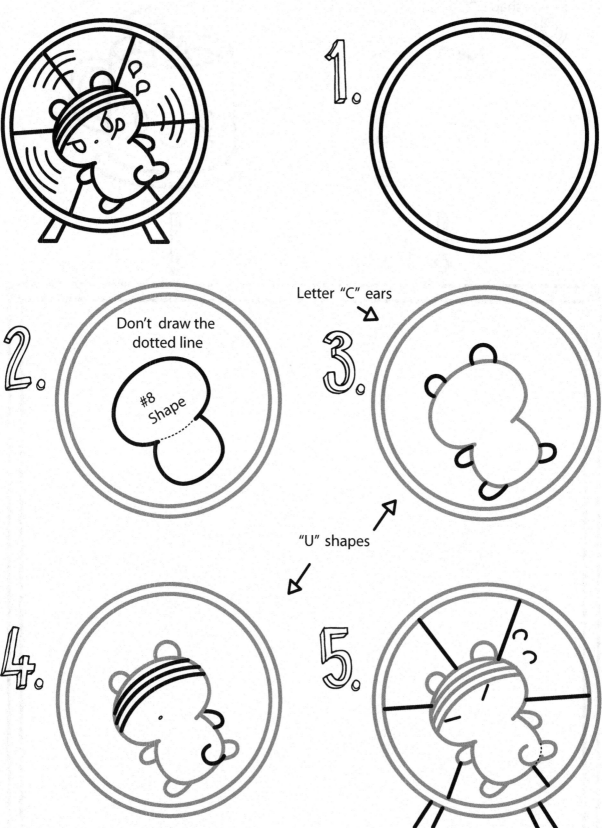

1.

2. Don't draw the dotted line

#8 Shape

3. Letter "C" ears

"U" shapes

4.

5.

6.

Don't draw the dotted line

"p" mouth

NOW YOU TRY

SOME FREEBIE PAGES FROM MY OTHER BOOKS

KISS THE BABY

Here is a paper
folding trick in which
you can choose from
two different pictures ...
(1) The mom and dad kiss or
(2) Mom and Dad hold and
kiss the baby.

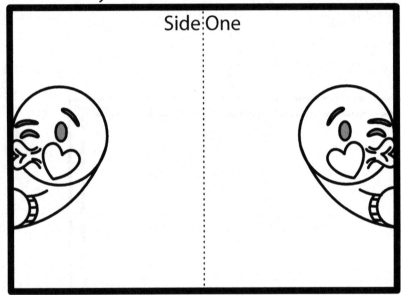

Side One

1.

Get a piece of paper. On
the first side of the paper,
draw the two characters
that you see to the left.
Below find the tutorial
for drawing each
character. Draw one on
the left and one on the right.

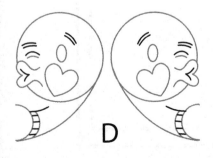

A

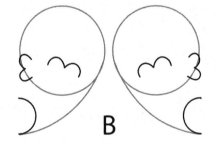

B

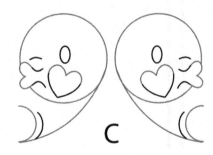

C

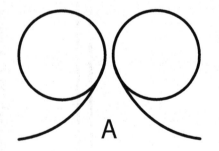

D

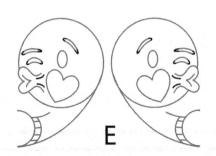

E

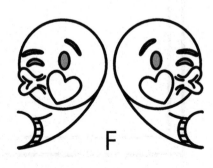

F

Side Two

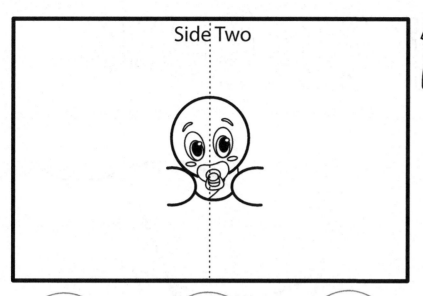

2. On the 2nd side of the paper, draw the baby that you see to the left. Below find the lesson for drawing the baby.

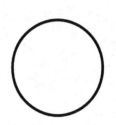

4.

If you close the paper completely, the parents are hugging and kissing.

3. Curl the paper so that the baby is on the inside. Match up the hands on the parents with the hands holding the baby.

FROM MY COOL STUFF EMOJI BOOK

How to Draw Cool Stuff, Emojis, 3D
Emoji Faces and Things
HOW TO DRAW COOL 3D EMOJI STUFF FOR OLDER KIDS, TEENS, TEACHERS, AND STUDENTS
BY RACHEL A GOLDSTEIN

LETTER F DUCKLING

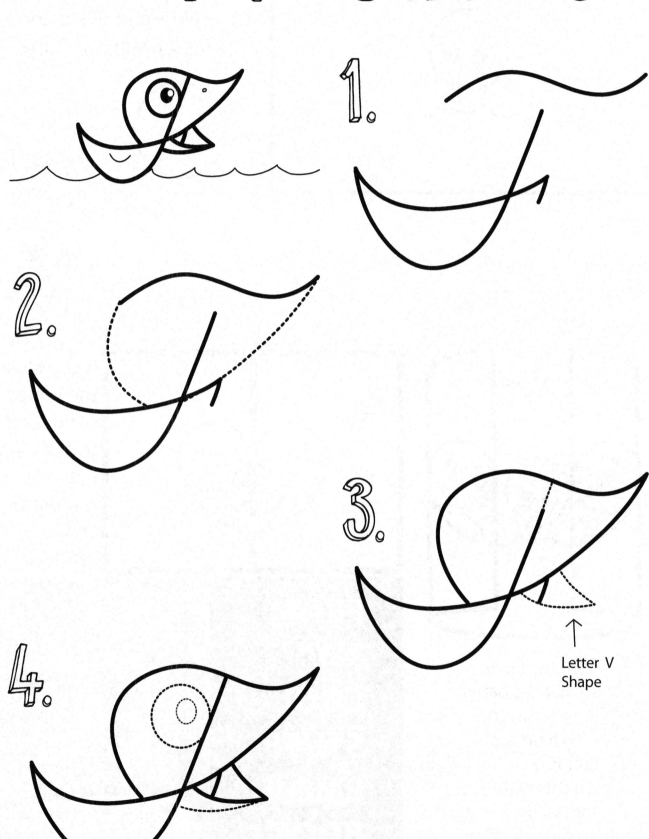

1.

2.

3.

Letter V
Shape

4.

5.

↓ NOW YOU TRY ↓

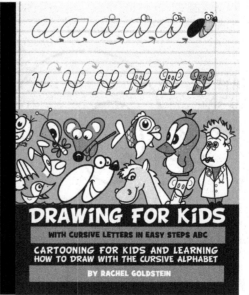

FROM
MY
CURSIVE
DRAWING
BOOK

DRAWING FOR KIDS
WITH CURSIVE LETTERS IN EASY STEPS ABC
CARTOONING FOR KIDS AND LEARNING
HOW TO DRAW WITH THE CURSIVE ALPHABET
BY RACHEL GOLDSTEIN

TEN BIRDIE

1.

2.

3.

4.

5.

6.

NOW YOU TRY

FROM
MY
NUMBER
DRAWING
BOOK

ENERGETIC LITTLE BOY

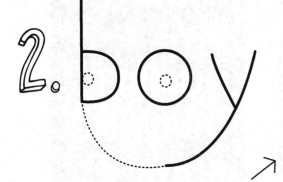

1. boy

2. boy

Letter M Shaped Zig-Zags

3.

4.

5.

BOX RISING OFF OF PAPER

Here is a cool 3-dimensional effect that is quite simple to draw. It really will look like a cute square is rising off of the paper.

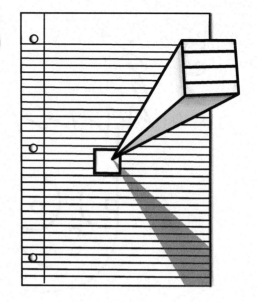

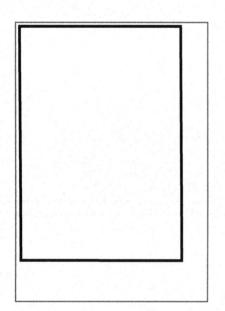

1. Draw a rectangle on the upper left side of a piece of paper.

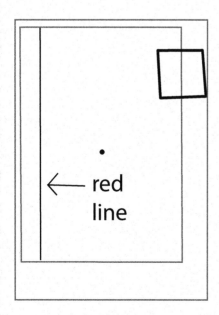

← red line

2. Draw a light red line along the left side of the rectangle. Draw slightly slanted rectangle on right side. Draw a dot on the page.

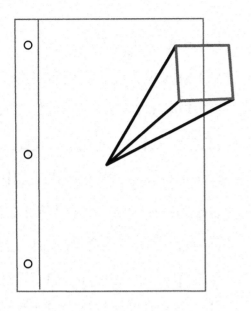

3. Draw lines from the rectangle down to the point you drew. Draw 3 circles on left side of page.

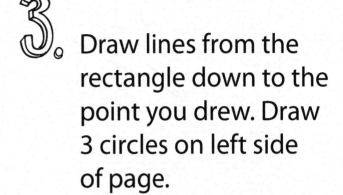

blue lines →

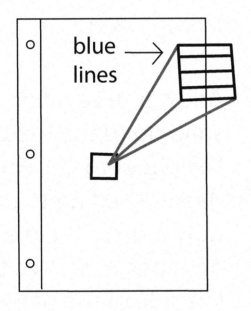

4. Draw a smaller rectangle around the point. Draw 3 blue lines on the bigger rectangle.

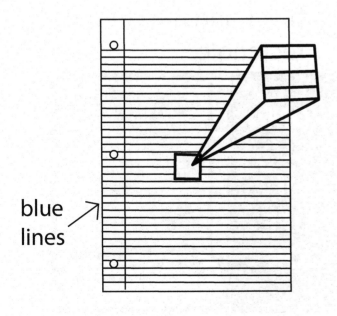

blue lines →

5. Draw blue lines around the shapes that you drew.

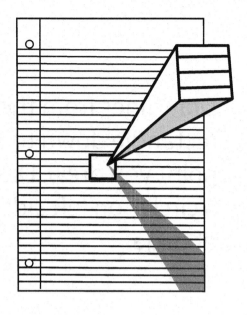

 Draw a gray cast shadow by drawing 2 outward slanted lines that form a triangle. Fill it in gray. You should be able to see the lines thru the shadow. Use a lighter gray to shade the right side of the paper tower.

Shade the left side of the holes + rectangle

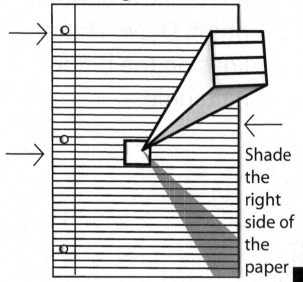

→

→

← Shade the right side of the paper

7. Add some very light shading to the top of the paper tower. Add darker shading to the right side of the piece of paper, as well as the left side of the paper holes and the cut out rectangle.

FROM MY COOL STUFF BOOK

How to Draw Cool Things, Optical Illusions, 3D Letters, Cartoons and Stuff
A COOL DRAWING GUIDE FOR OLDER KIDS, TEENS, TEACHERS, AND STUDENTS
BY RACHEL GOLDSTEIN

PAPERCLIP PROMPT

Use the boring paperclip picture (on the next page) to start your imagination churning. Below is an example drawing...but imagine up your own picture!

DRAWING TELEPHONE

Have you ever played telephone? It is a fun game where the first player in the circle whispers a word into the ear of the person sitting to their right. Players whisper the word to their neighbors until it reaches the last player in line. Then the first and last player compare their words to see if it was relayed correctly.

Well in Drawing Telephone, words are replaced with drawings - as you probably have guessed. Here is how to play the game:

Man

The first player writes down a word on a notepad

The notebook is handed to the player to the right. This player secretly looks at the word, then turns to the next page and draws a picture of that word.

3.

Monkey

The notebook is passed to the next person to the right. This player examines the picture and then writes down what he/she thinks the word is on the next page.

4.

The notebook is handed to the player to the right. This player secretly looks at the word, then turns to the next page and draws a picture of that word.

5.

Ferret

6.

And it continues on until the last person.

7.

Man

Compare the first word and the last picture to see if they match!